**nickelodeon**™

降击神通

# AVATAR

## THE LAST AIRBENDER™

Created by
**Bryan Konietzko**
**Michael Dante DiMartino**

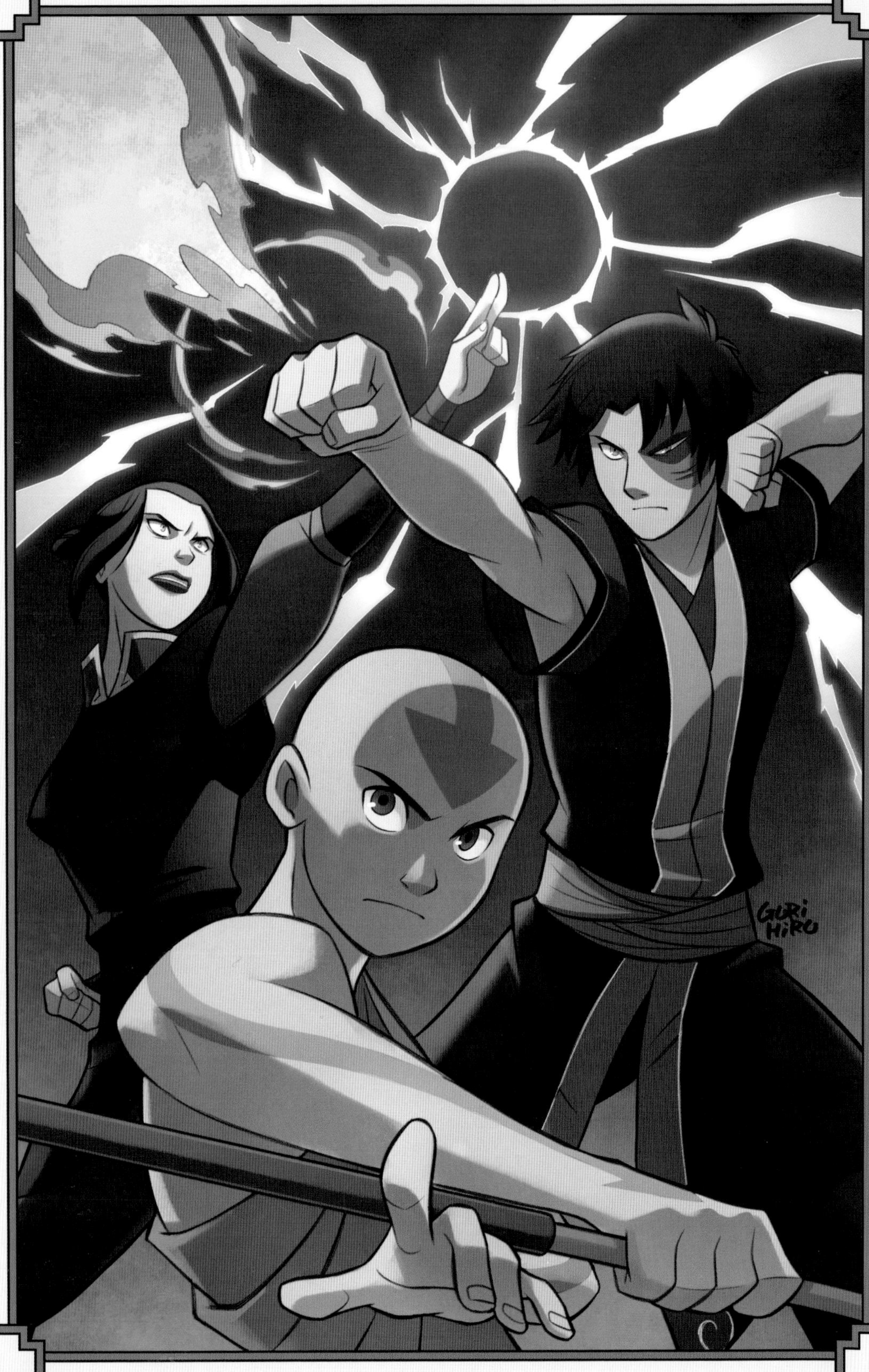
GURI HIRU

publisher
**MIKE RICHARDSON**

collection designer
**JUSTIN COUCH**

assistant editors
**IAN TUCKER** and **AARON WALKER**

editor
**DAVE MARSHALL**

Special thanks to Linda Lee,
Kat van Dam, James Salerno, and Joan Hilty
at Nickelodeon, and to Bryan Konietzko
and Michael Dante DiMartino.

Published by
**Dark Horse Books**
A division of
Dark Horse Comics LLC
10956 SE Main Street
Milwaukie, OR 97222

**DarkHorse.com**
**Nick.com**

International Licensing: (503) 905-2377
To find a comics shop in your area, visit comicshoplocator.com

First edition: October 2013
ISBN 978-1-61655-184-1

7 9 10 8 6

# AVATAR
## THE LAST AIRBENDER

### THE SEARCH · PART THREE

script
**GENE LUEN YANG**

art and cover
**GURIHIRU**

lettering
**MICHAEL HEISLER**

DARK HORSE BOOKS

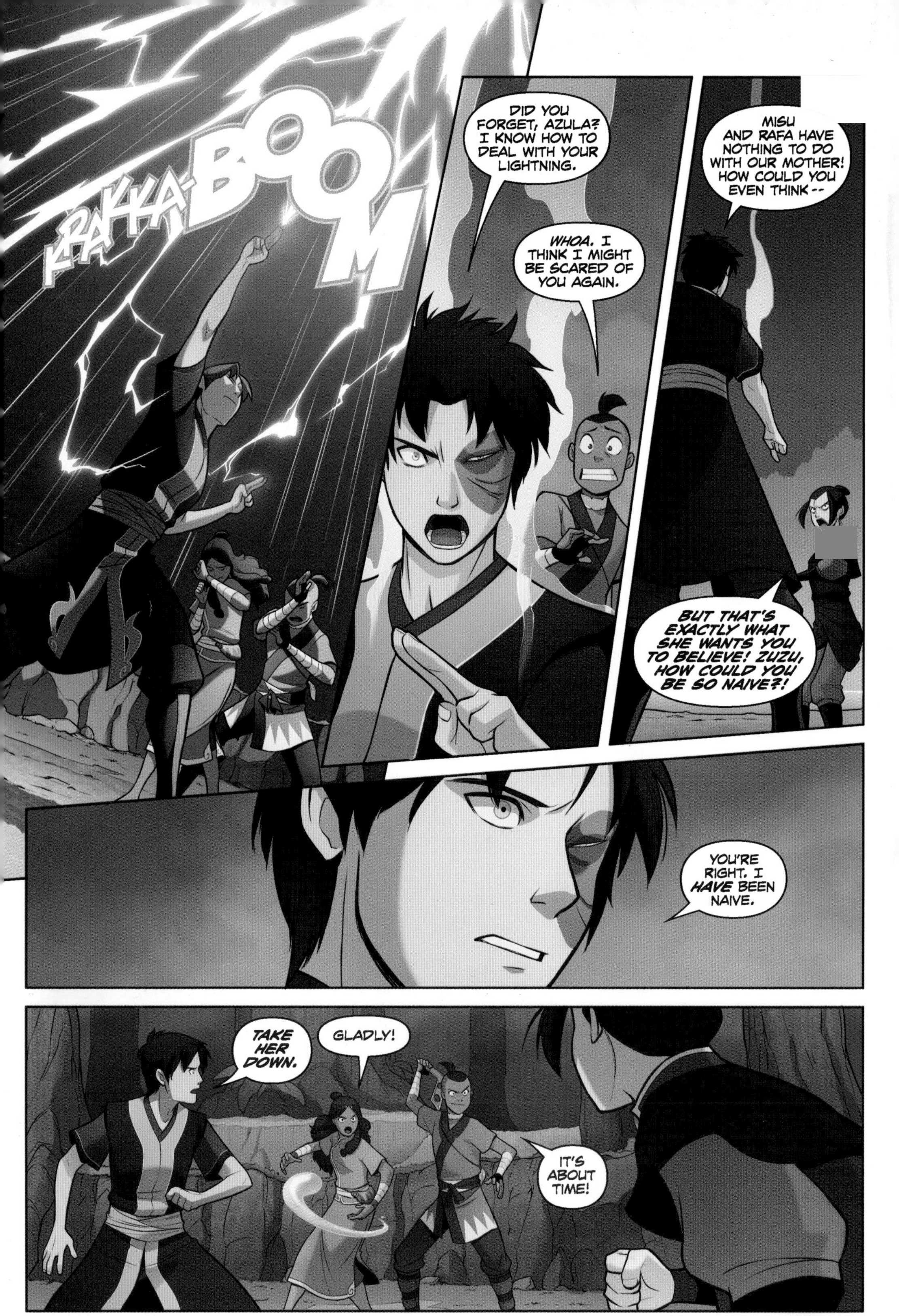
KRAKKA-BOOM
DID YOU FORGET, AZULA? I KNOW HOW TO DEAL WITH YOUR LIGHTNING.
WHOA. I THINK I MIGHT BE SCARED OF YOU AGAIN.
MISU AND RAFA HAVE NOTHING TO DO WITH OUR MOTHER! HOW COULD YOU EVEN THINK --
BUT THAT'S EXACTLY WHAT SHE WANTS YOU TO BELIEVE! ZUZU, HOW COULD YOU BE SO NAIVE?!
YOU'RE RIGHT. I HAVE BEEN NAIVE.
TAKE HER DOWN.
GLADLY!
IT'S ABOUT TIME!

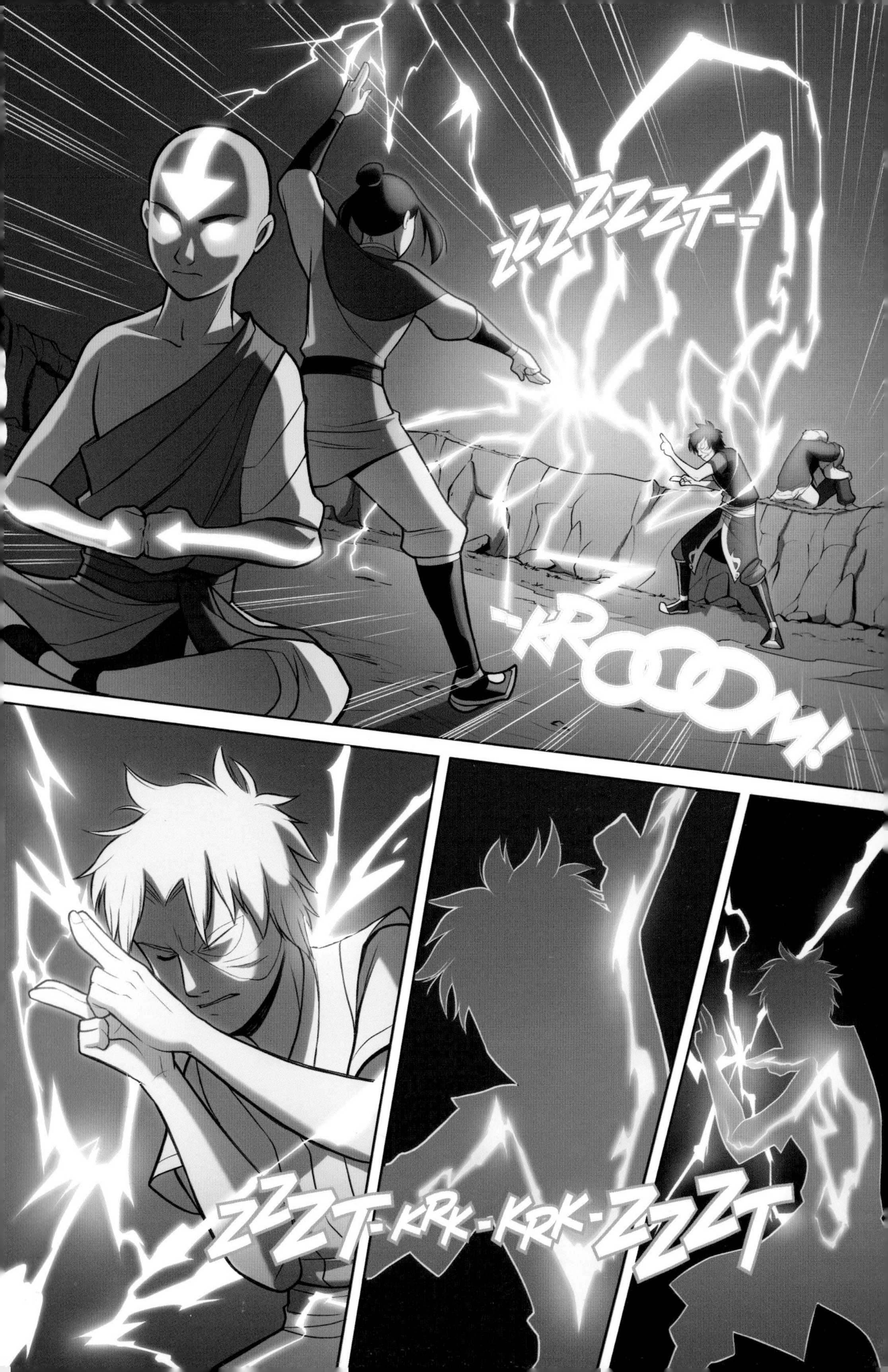
ZZZZZZZT--
-KROOOOM!
ZZZZT-KRK-KRK-ZZZT

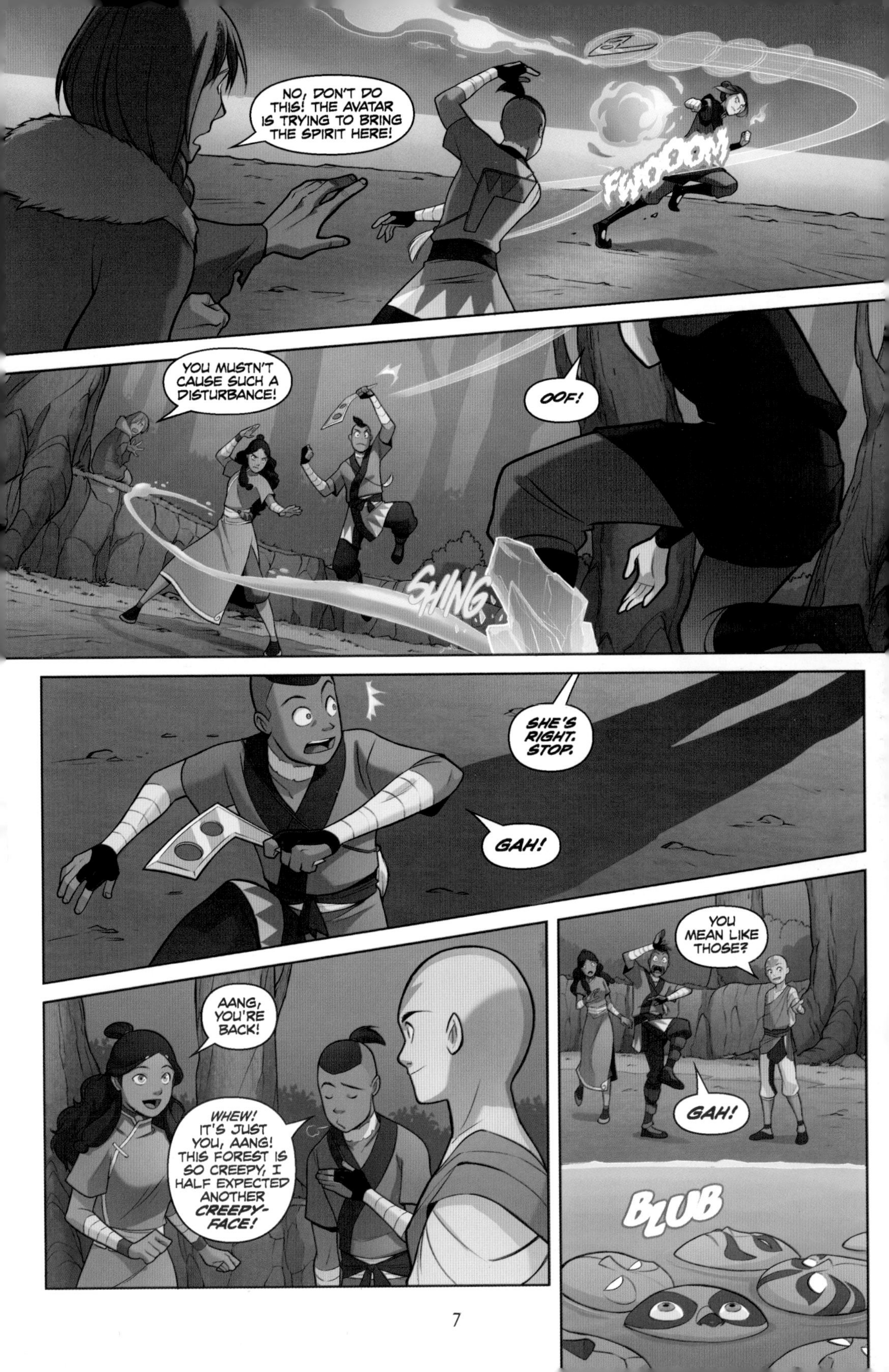
NO, DON'T DO THIS! THE AVATAR IS TRYING TO BRING THE SPIRIT HERE!
FWOOOM
YOU MUSTN'T CAUSE SUCH A DISTURBANCE!
OOF!
SHING
SHE'S RIGHT. STOP.
GAH!
AANG, YOU'RE BACK!
WHEW! IT'S JUST YOU, AANG! THIS FOREST IS SO CREEPY, I HALF EXPECTED ANOTHER CREEPY-FACE!
YOU MEAN LIKE THOSE?
GAH!
BLUB

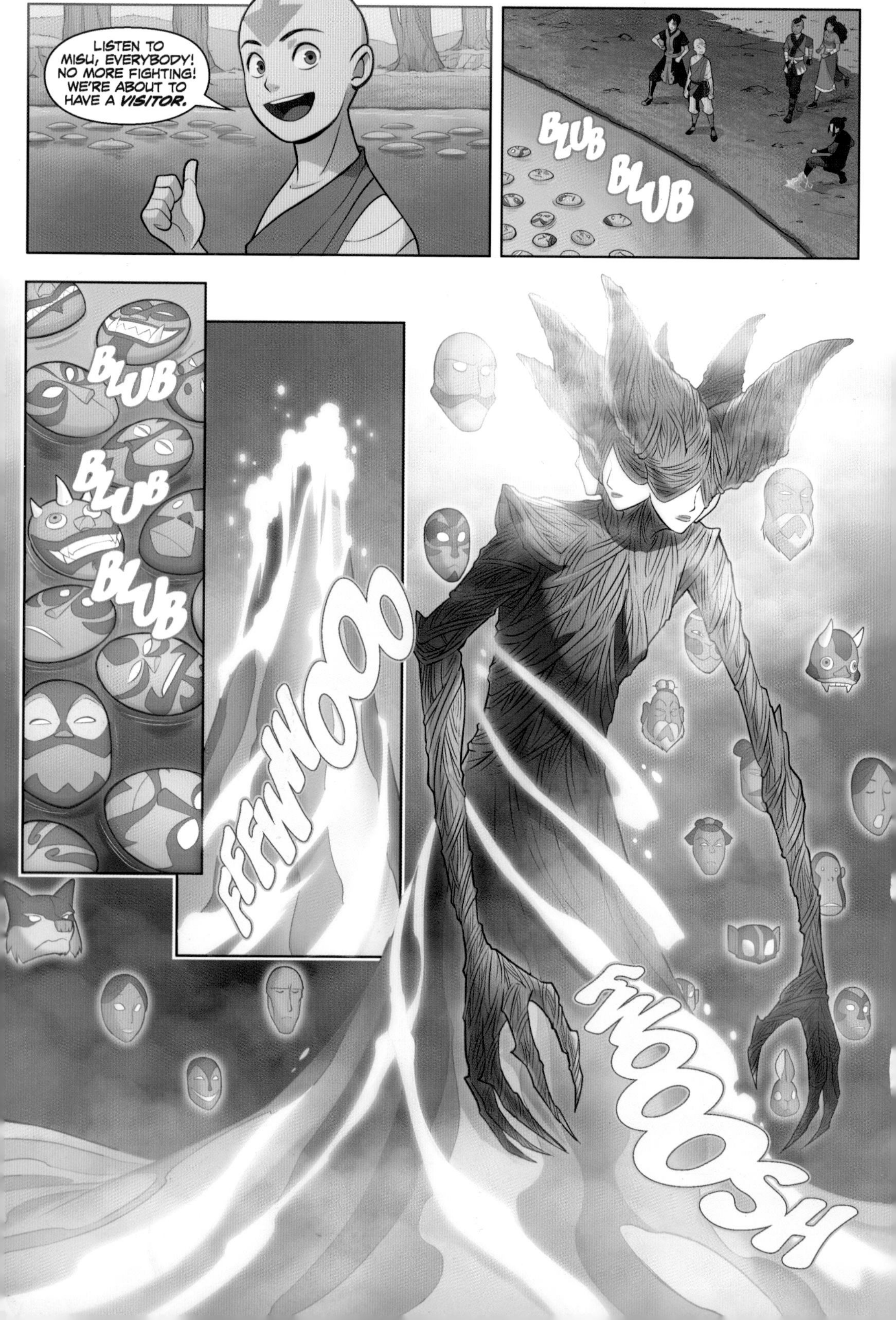
LISTEN TO MISU, EVERYBODY! NO MORE FIGHTING! WE'RE ABOUT TO HAVE A VISITOR.
BLUB
BLUB
BLUB
BLUB
BLUB
FFFWOOO
FWOOOSH

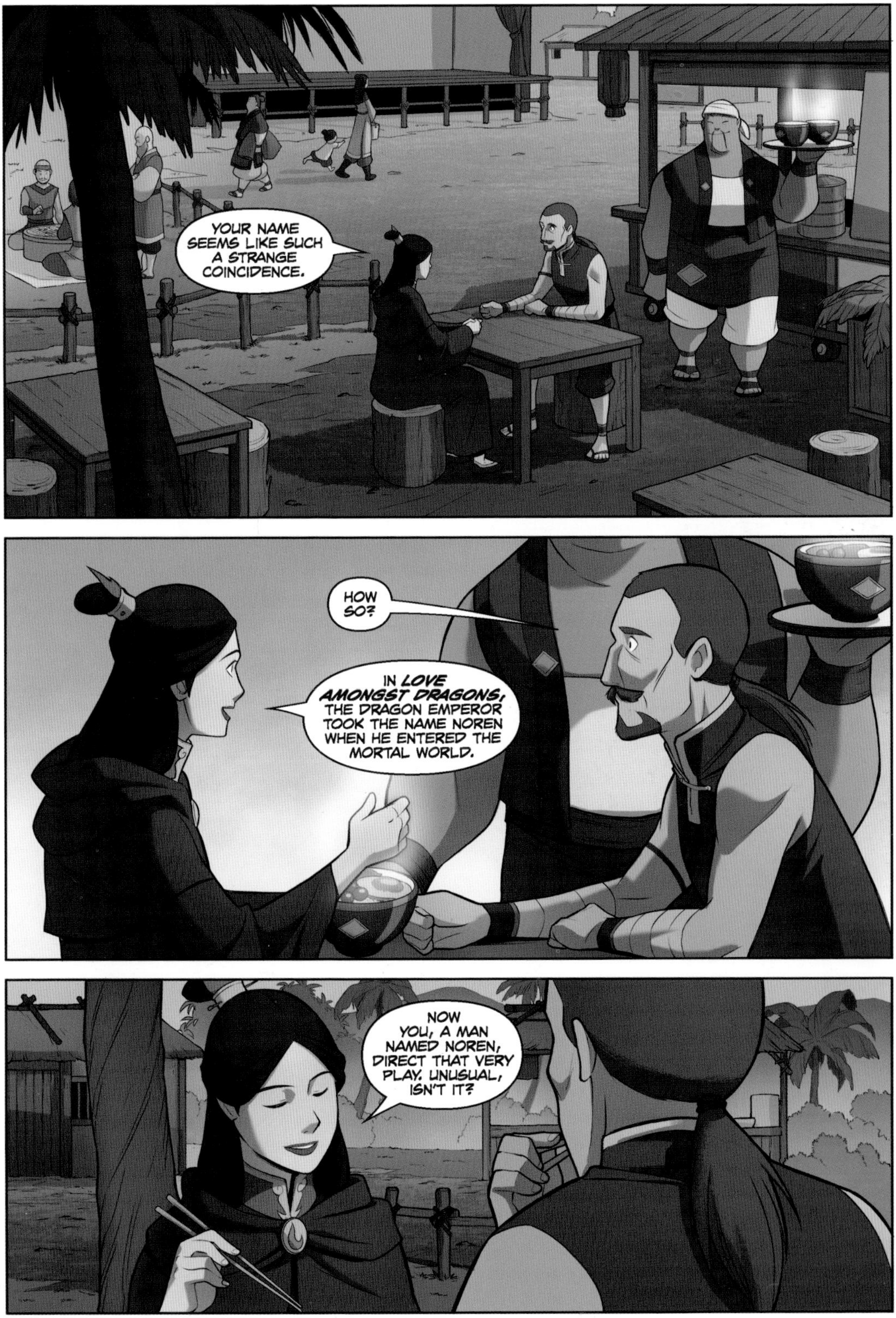
YOUR NAME SEEMS LIKE SUCH A STRANGE COINCIDENCE.
HOW SO?
IN *LOVE AMONGST DRAGONS,* THE DRAGON EMPEROR TOOK THE NAME NOREN WHEN HE ENTERED THE MORTAL WORLD.
NOW YOU, A MAN NAMED NOREN, DIRECT THAT VERY PLAY. UNUSUAL, ISN'T IT?

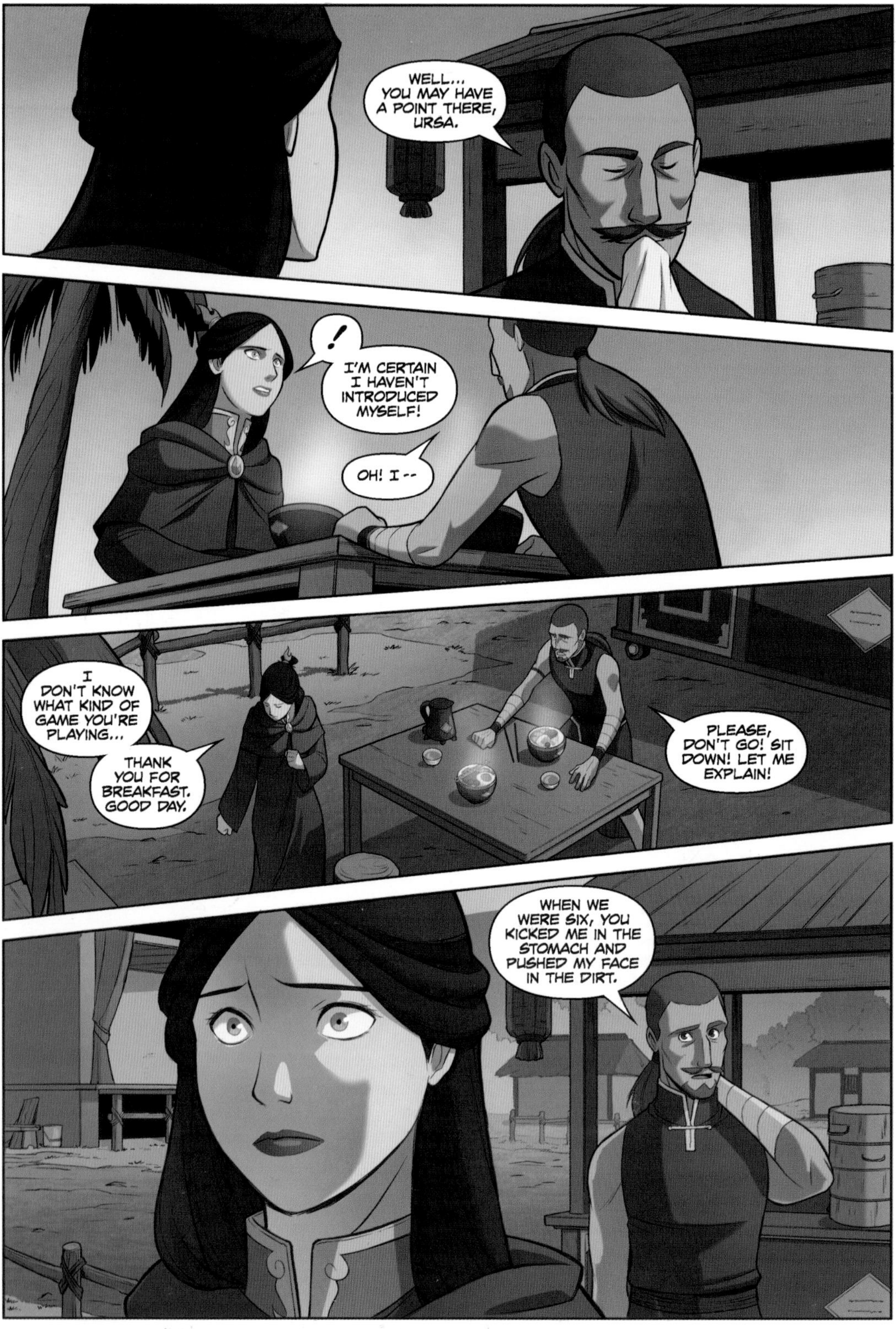
WELL... YOU MAY HAVE A POINT THERE, URSA.
!
I'M CERTAIN I HAVEN'T INTRODUCED MYSELF!
OH! I --
I DON'T KNOW WHAT KIND OF GAME YOU'RE PLAYING...
THANK YOU FOR BREAKFAST. GOOD DAY.
PLEASE, DON'T GO! SIT DOWN! LET ME EXPLAIN!
WHEN WE WERE SIX, YOU KICKED ME IN THE STOMACH AND PUSHED MY FACE IN THE DIRT.

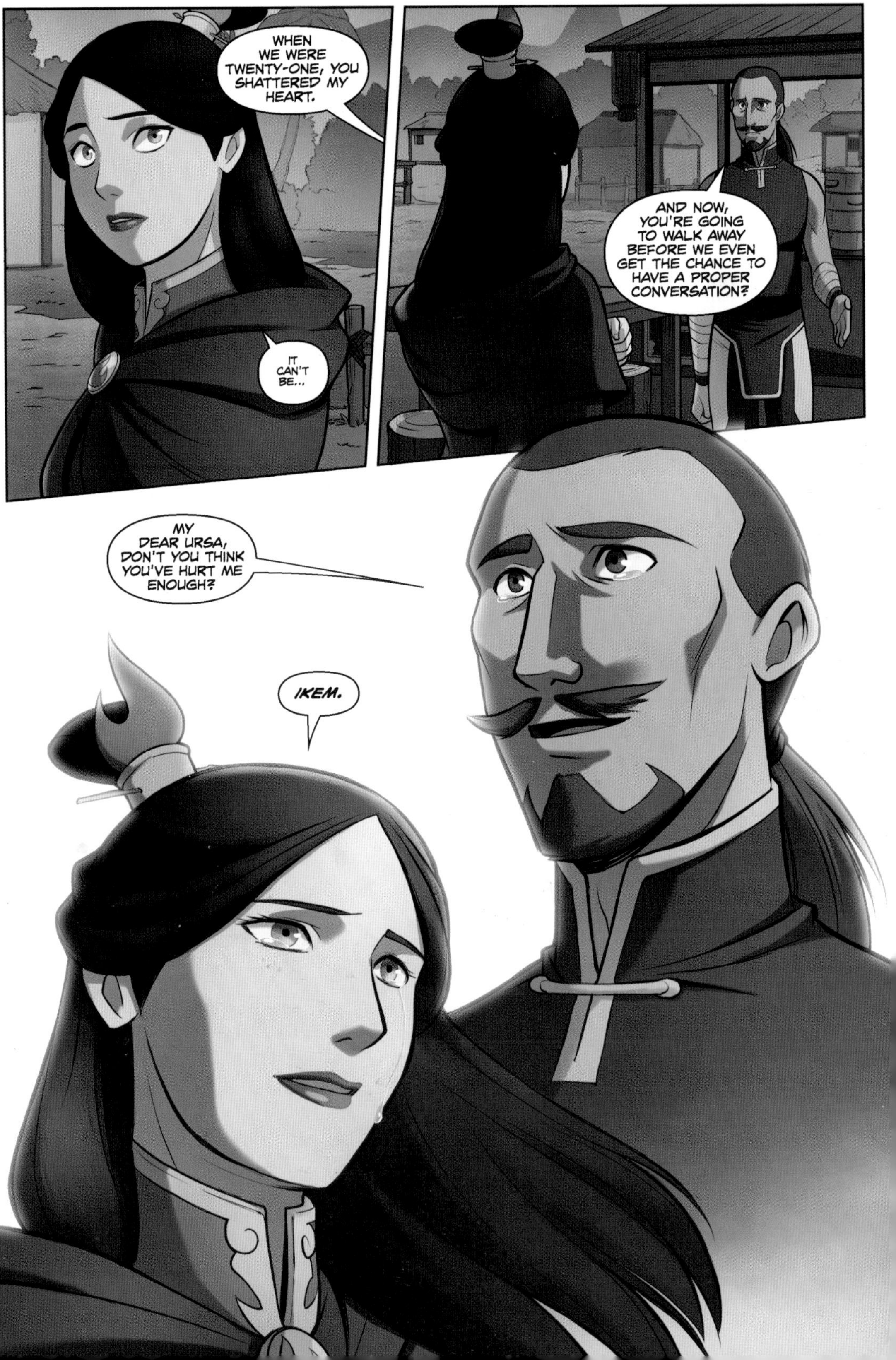
WHEN WE WERE TWENTY-ONE, YOU SHATTERED MY HEART.
IT CAN'T BE...
AND NOW, YOU'RE GOING TO WALK AWAY BEFORE WE EVEN GET THE CHANCE TO HAVE A PROPER CONVERSATION?
MY DEAR URSA, DON'T YOU THINK YOU'VE HURT ME ENOUGH?
IKEM.

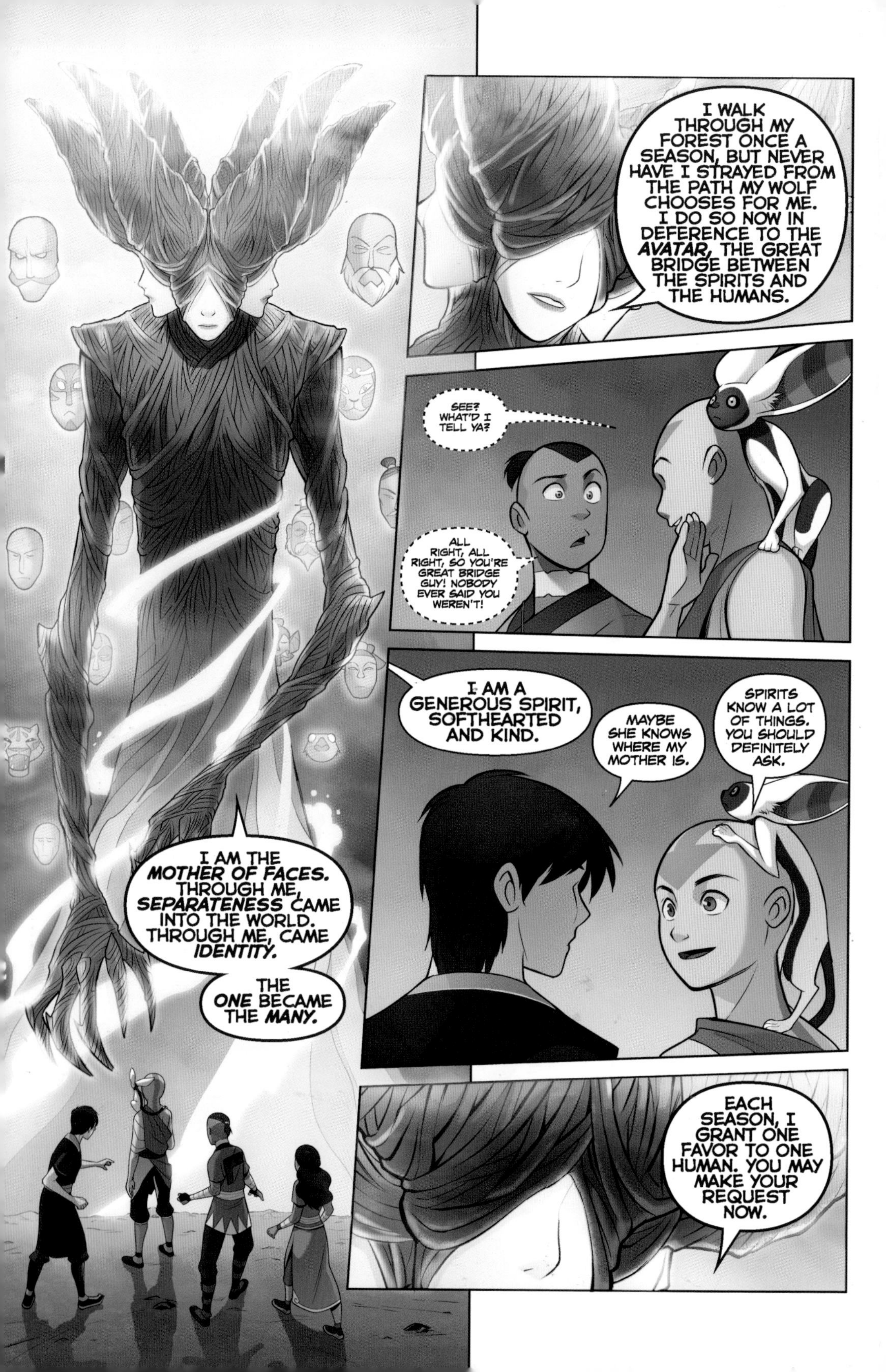
I AM THE MOTHER OF FACES. THROUGH ME, SEPARATENESS CAME INTO THE WORLD. THROUGH ME, CAME IDENTITY.
THE ONE BECAME THE MANY.
I WALK THROUGH MY FOREST ONCE A SEASON, BUT NEVER HAVE I STRAYED FROM THE PATH MY WOLF CHOOSES FOR ME. I DO SO NOW IN DEFERENCE TO THE AVATAR, THE GREAT BRIDGE BETWEEN THE SPIRITS AND THE HUMANS.
SEE? WHAT'D I TELL YA?
ALL RIGHT, ALL RIGHT, SO YOU'RE GREAT BRIDGE GUY! NOBODY EVER SAID YOU WEREN'T!
I AM A GENEROUS SPIRIT, SOFTHEARTED AND KIND.
MAYBE SHE KNOWS WHERE MY MOTHER IS.
SPIRITS KNOW A LOT OF THINGS. YOU SHOULD DEFINITELY ASK.
EACH SEASON, I GRANT ONE FAVOR TO ONE HUMAN. YOU MAY MAKE YOUR REQUEST NOW.

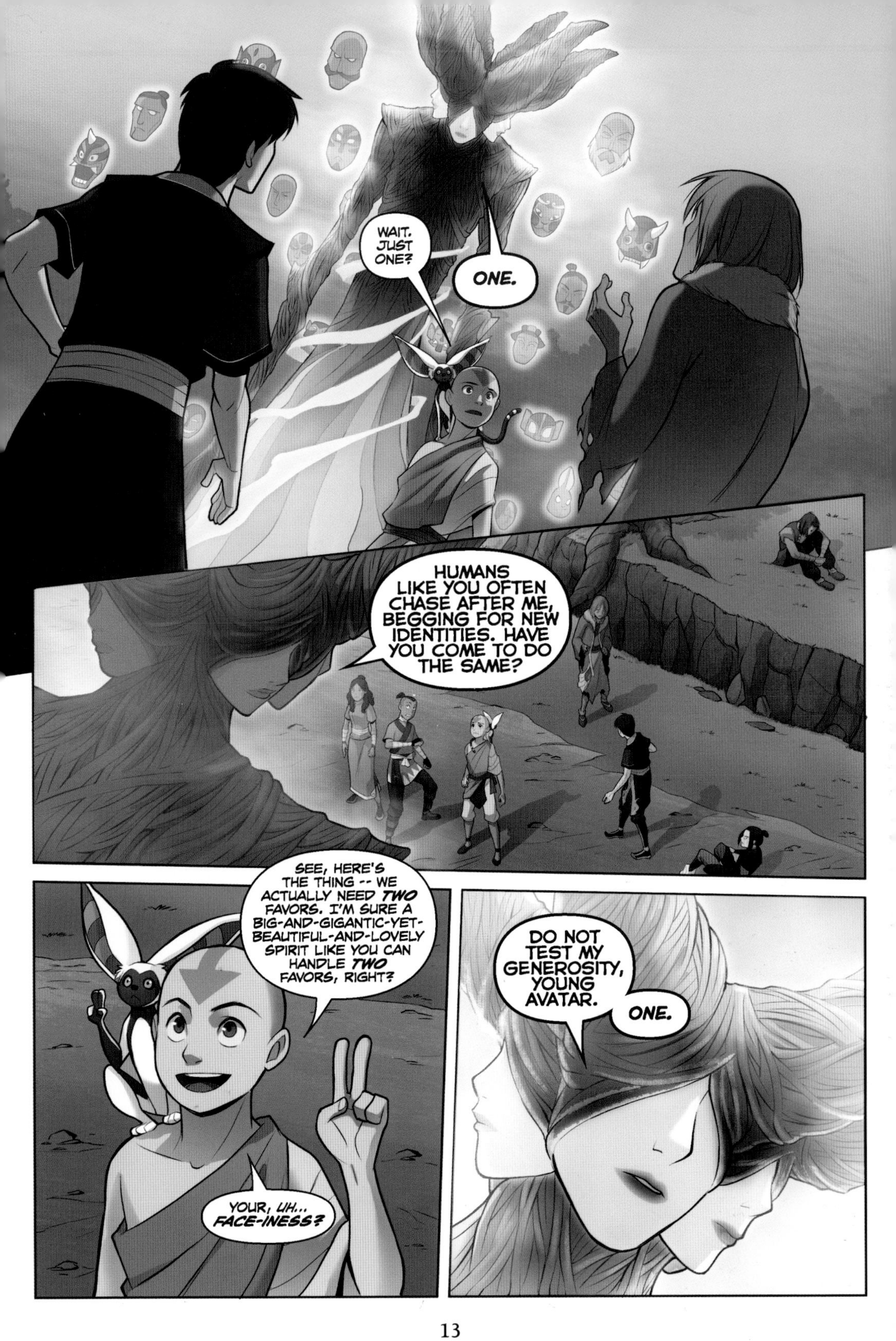
WAIT. JUST ONE?
ONE.
HUMANS LIKE YOU OFTEN CHASE AFTER ME, BEGGING FOR NEW IDENTITIES. HAVE YOU COME TO DO THE SAME?
SEE, HERE'S THE THING -- WE ACTUALLY NEED *TWO* FAVORS. I'M SURE A BIG-AND-GIGANTIC-YET-BEAUTIFUL-AND-LOVELY SPIRIT LIKE YOU CAN HANDLE *TWO* FAVORS, RIGHT?
YOUR, UH... *FACE-INESS?*
DO NOT TEST MY GENEROSITY, YOUNG AVATAR.
ONE.

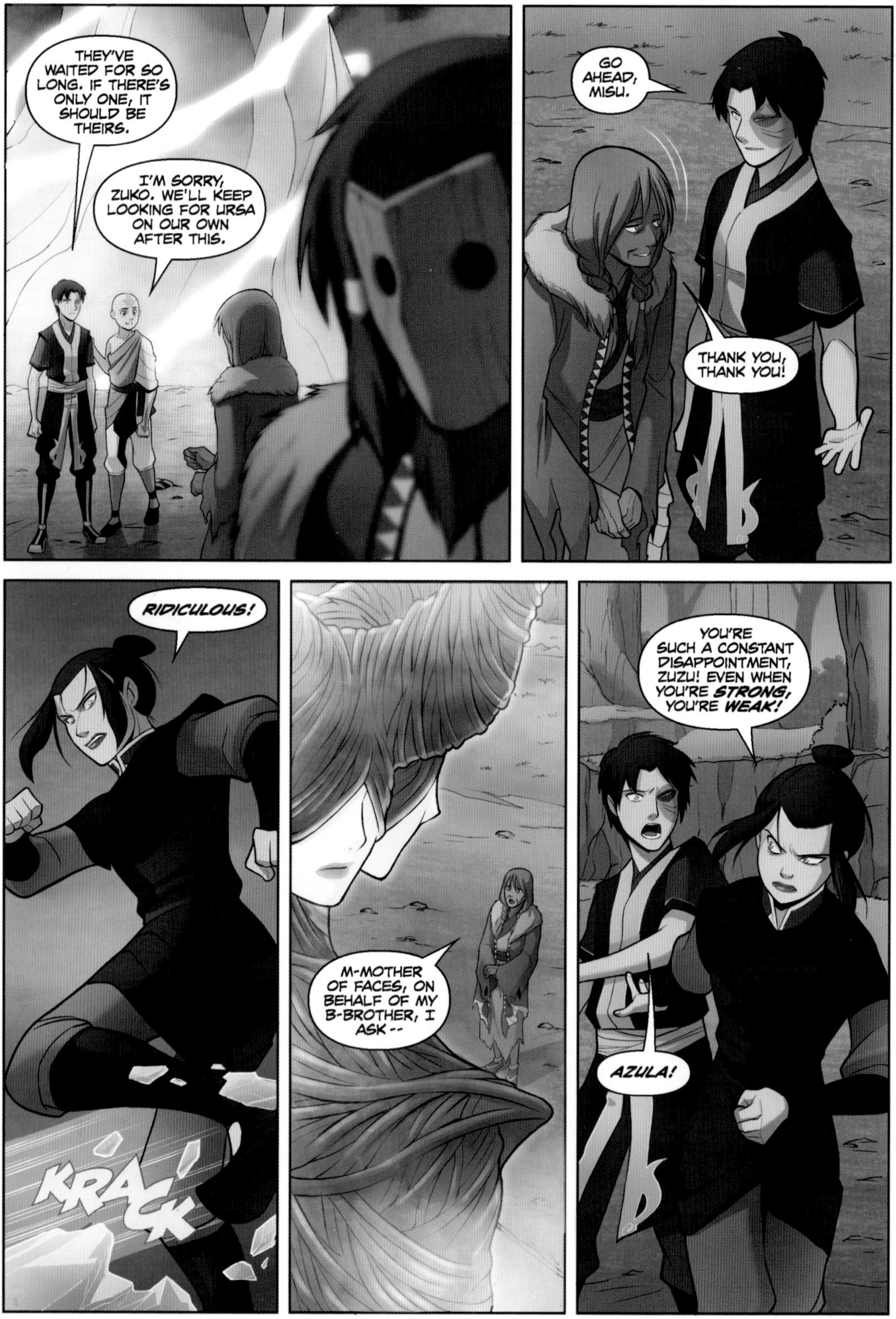
THEY'VE WAITED FOR SO LONG. IF THERE'S ONLY ONE, IT SHOULD BE THEIRS.
I'M SORRY, ZUKO. WE'LL KEEP LOOKING FOR URSA ON OUR OWN AFTER THIS.
GO AHEAD, MISU.
THANK YOU, THANK YOU!
RIDICULOUS!
KRACK
M-MOTHER OF FACES, ON BEHALF OF MY B-BROTHER, I ASK --
YOU'RE SUCH A CONSTANT DISAPPOINTMENT, ZUZU! EVEN WHEN YOU'RE STRONG, YOU'RE WEAK!
AZULA!

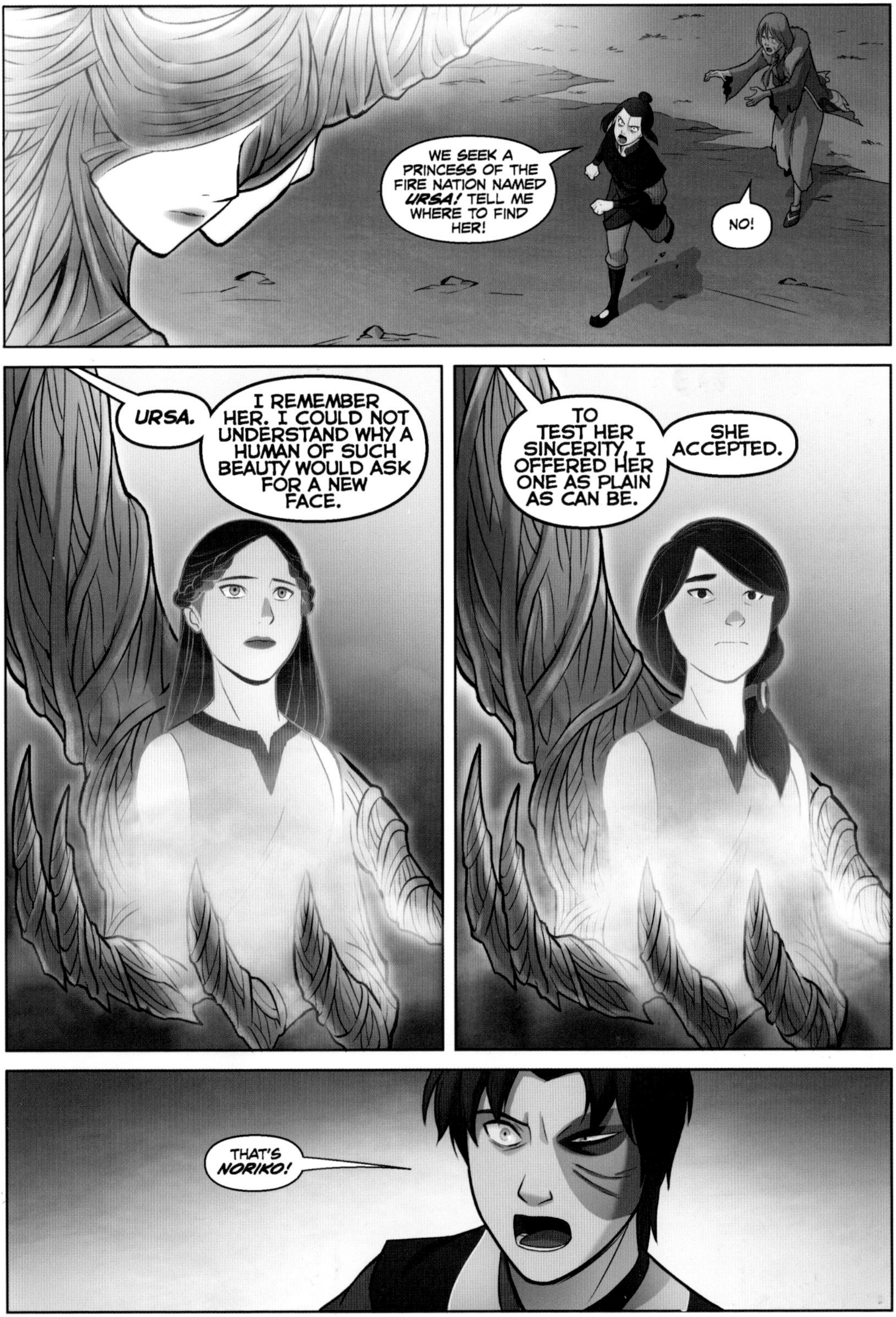
WE SEEK A PRINCESS OF THE FIRE NATION NAMED URSA! TELL ME WHERE TO FIND HER!
NO!
URSA.
I REMEMBER HER. I COULD NOT UNDERSTAND WHY A HUMAN OF SUCH BEAUTY WOULD ASK FOR A NEW FACE.
TO TEST HER SINCERITY, I OFFERED HER ONE AS PLAIN AS CAN BE.
SHE ACCEPTED.
THAT'S NORIKO!

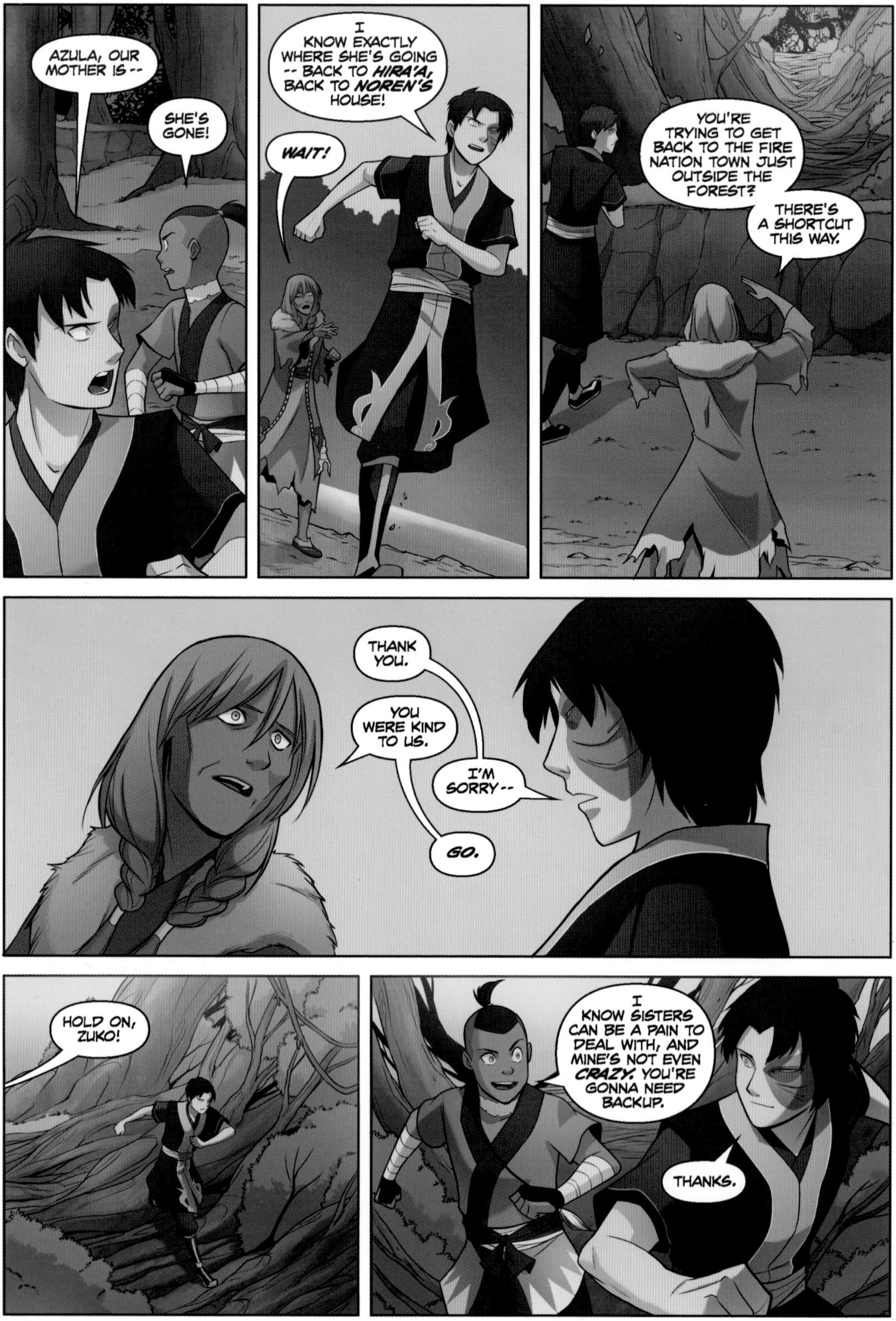
AZULA, OUR MOTHER IS --
SHE'S GONE!
I KNOW EXACTLY WHERE SHE'S GOING -- BACK TO HIRA'A, BACK TO NOREN'S HOUSE!
WAIT!
YOU'RE TRYING TO GET BACK TO THE FIRE NATION TOWN JUST OUTSIDE THE FOREST?
THERE'S A SHORTCUT THIS WAY.
THANK YOU.
YOU WERE KIND TO US.
I'M SORRY --
GO.
HOLD ON, ZUKO!
I KNOW SISTERS CAN BE A PAIN TO DEAL WITH, AND MINE'S NOT EVEN CRAZY. YOU'RE GONNA NEED BACKUP.
THANKS.

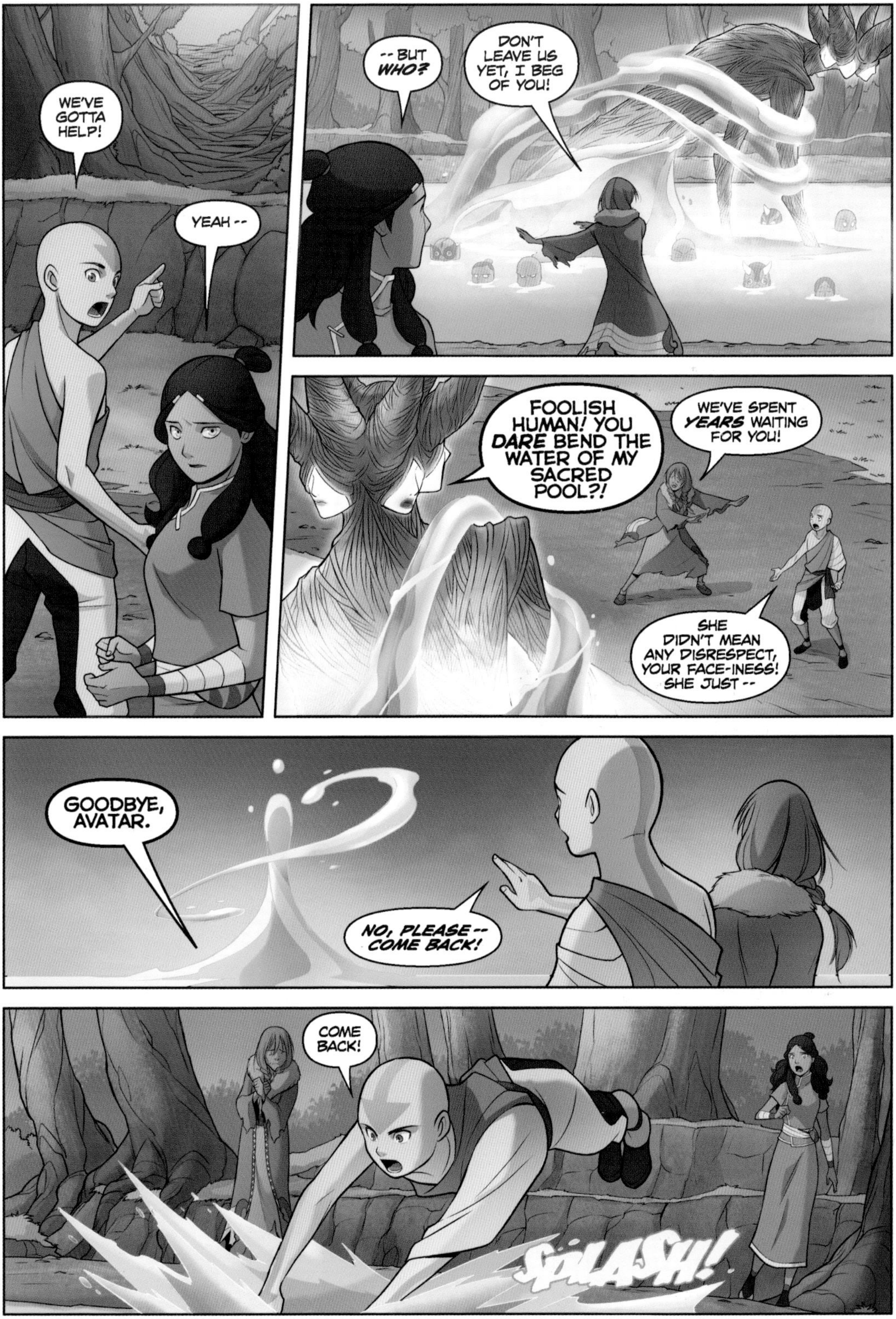
WE'VE GOTTA HELP!
YEAH --
-- BUT WHO?
DON'T LEAVE US YET, I BEG OF YOU!
FOOLISH HUMAN! YOU DARE BEND THE WATER OF MY SACRED POOL?!
WE'VE SPENT YEARS WAITING FOR YOU!
SHE DIDN'T MEAN ANY DISRESPECT, YOUR FACE-INESS! SHE JUST --
GOODBYE, AVATAR.
NO, PLEASE -- COME BACK!
COME BACK!
SPLASH!

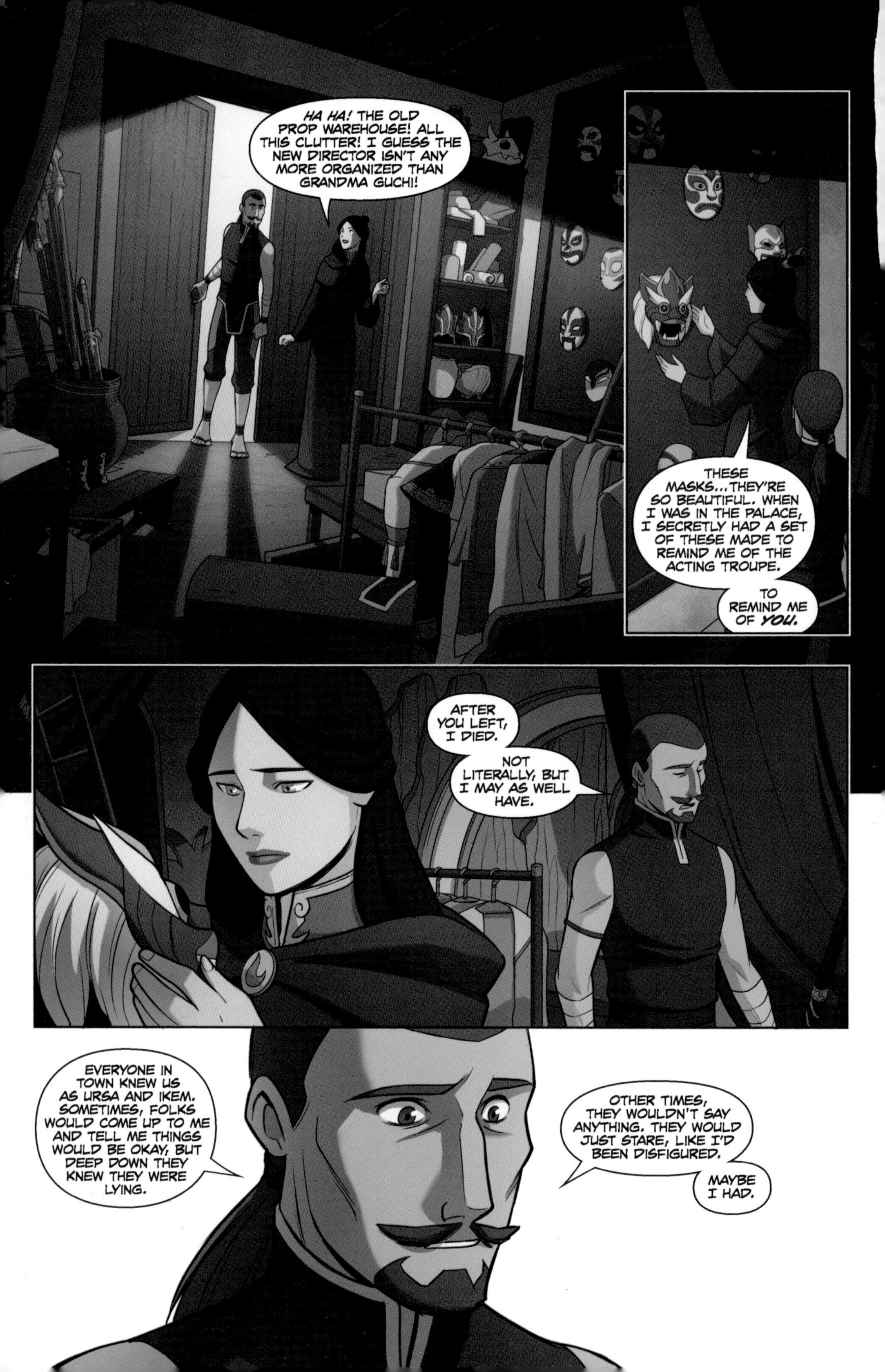
HA HA! THE OLD PROP WAREHOUSE! ALL THIS CLUTTER! I GUESS THE NEW DIRECTOR ISN'T ANY MORE ORGANIZED THAN GRANDMA GUCHI!
THESE MASKS... THEY'RE SO BEAUTIFUL. WHEN I WAS IN THE PALACE, I SECRETLY HAD A SET OF THESE MADE TO REMIND ME OF THE ACTING TROUPE.
TO REMIND ME OF YOU.
AFTER YOU LEFT, I DIED.
NOT LITERALLY, BUT I MAY AS WELL HAVE.
EVERYONE IN TOWN KNEW US AS URSA AND IKEM. SOMETIMES, FOLKS WOULD COME UP TO ME AND TELL ME THINGS WOULD BE OKAY, BUT DEEP DOWN THEY KNEW THEY WERE LYING.
OTHER TIMES, THEY WOULDN'T SAY ANYTHING. THEY WOULD JUST STARE, LIKE I'D BEEN DISFIGURED.
MAYBE I HAD.

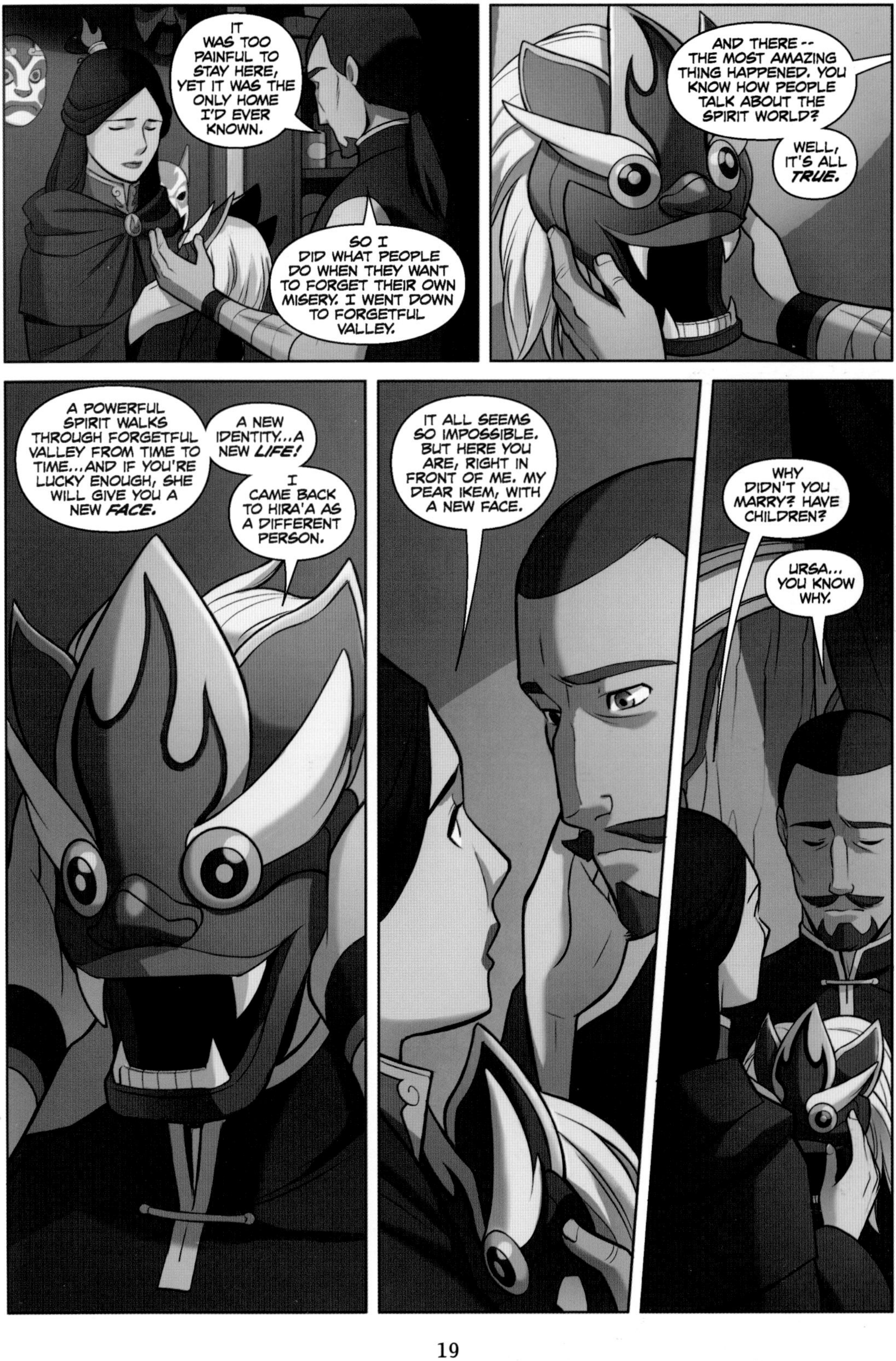
IT WAS TOO PAINFUL TO STAY HERE, YET IT WAS THE ONLY HOME I'D EVER KNOWN.
SO I DID WHAT PEOPLE DO WHEN THEY WANT TO FORGET THEIR OWN MISERY. I WENT DOWN TO FORGETFUL VALLEY.
AND THERE -- THE MOST AMAZING THING HAPPENED. YOU KNOW HOW PEOPLE TALK ABOUT THE SPIRIT WORLD?
WELL, IT'S ALL *TRUE.*
A POWERFUL SPIRIT WALKS THROUGH FORGETFUL VALLEY FROM TIME TO TIME...AND IF YOU'RE LUCKY ENOUGH, SHE WILL GIVE YOU A NEW *FACE.*
A NEW IDENTITY...A NEW *LIFE!*
I CAME BACK TO HIRA'A AS A DIFFERENT PERSON.
IT ALL SEEMS SO IMPOSSIBLE. BUT HERE YOU ARE, RIGHT IN FRONT OF ME. MY DEAR IKEM, WITH A NEW FACE.
WHY DIDN'T YOU MARRY? HAVE CHILDREN?
URSA... YOU KNOW WHY.

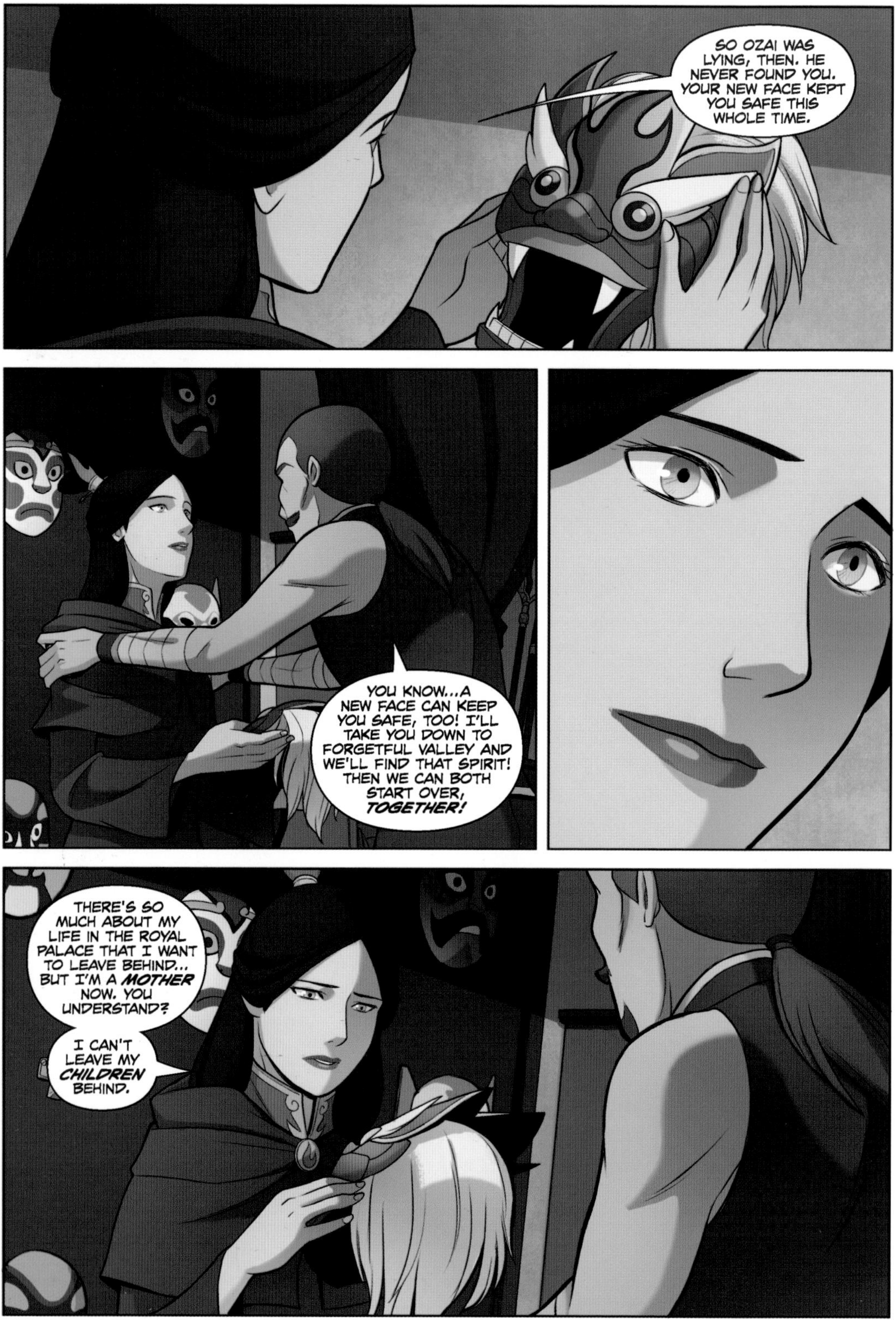
SO OZAI WAS LYING, THEN. HE NEVER FOUND YOU. YOUR NEW FACE KEPT YOU SAFE THIS WHOLE TIME.
YOU KNOW...A NEW FACE CAN KEEP YOU SAFE, TOO! I'LL TAKE YOU DOWN TO FORGETFUL VALLEY AND WE'LL FIND THAT SPIRIT! THEN WE CAN BOTH START OVER, TOGETHER!
THERE'S SO MUCH ABOUT MY LIFE IN THE ROYAL PALACE THAT I WANT TO LEAVE BEHIND... BUT I'M A MOTHER NOW. YOU UNDERSTAND?
I CAN'T LEAVE MY CHILDREN BEHIND.

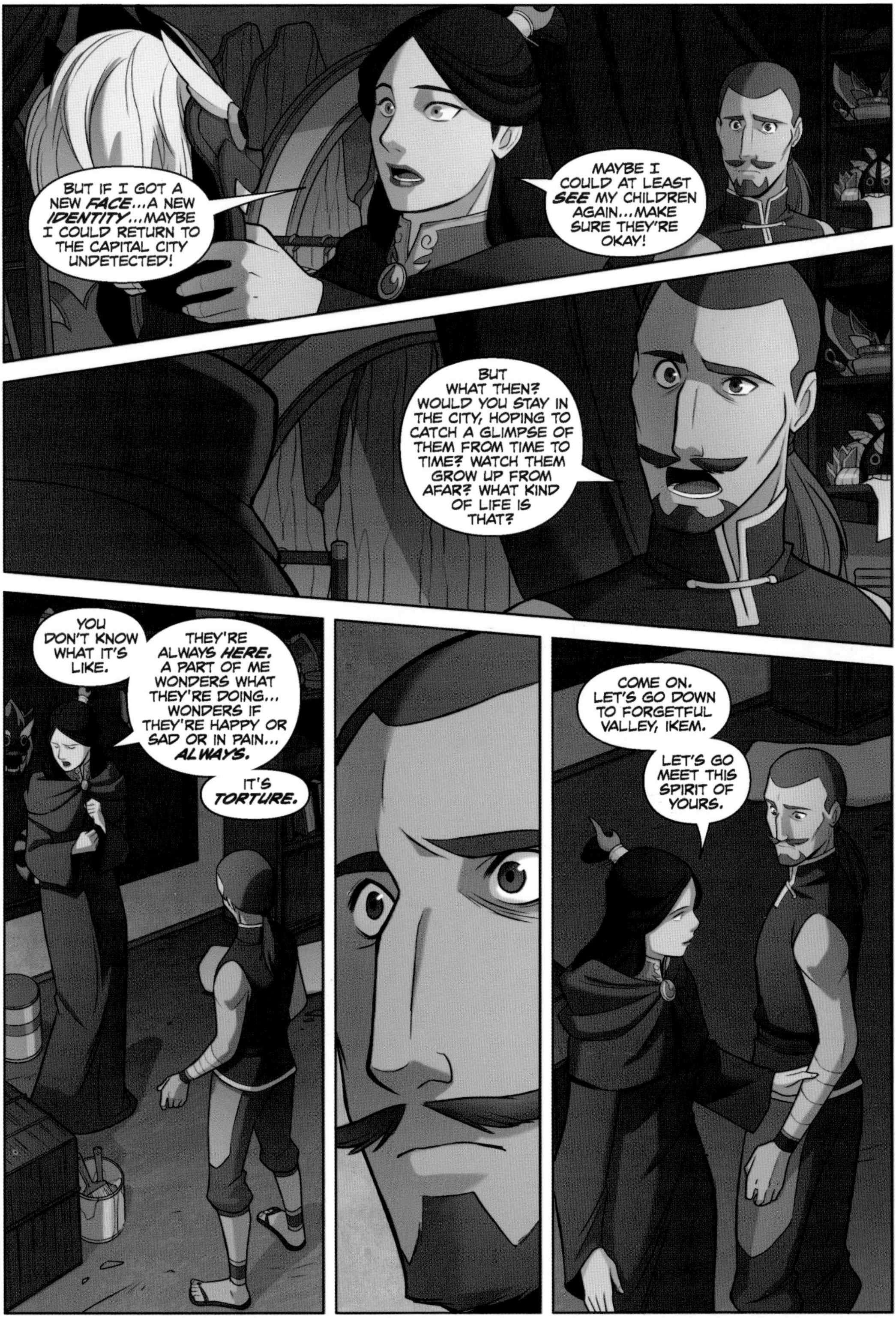

BUT IF I GOT A NEW *FACE*...A NEW *IDENTITY*...MAYBE I COULD RETURN TO THE CAPITAL CITY UNDETECTED!
MAYBE I COULD AT LEAST *SEE* MY CHILDREN AGAIN...MAKE SURE THEY'RE OKAY!
BUT WHAT THEN? WOULD YOU STAY IN THE CITY, HOPING TO CATCH A GLIMPSE OF THEM FROM TIME TO TIME? WATCH THEM GROW UP FROM AFAR? WHAT KIND OF LIFE IS THAT?
YOU DON'T KNOW WHAT IT'S LIKE.
THEY'RE ALWAYS *HERE.* A PART OF ME WONDERS WHAT THEY'RE DOING... WONDERS IF THEY'RE HAPPY OR SAD OR IN PAIN... *ALWAYS.*
IT'S *TORTURE.*
COME ON. LET'S GO DOWN TO FORGETFUL VALLEY, IKEM.
LET'S GO MEET THIS SPIRIT OF YOURS.

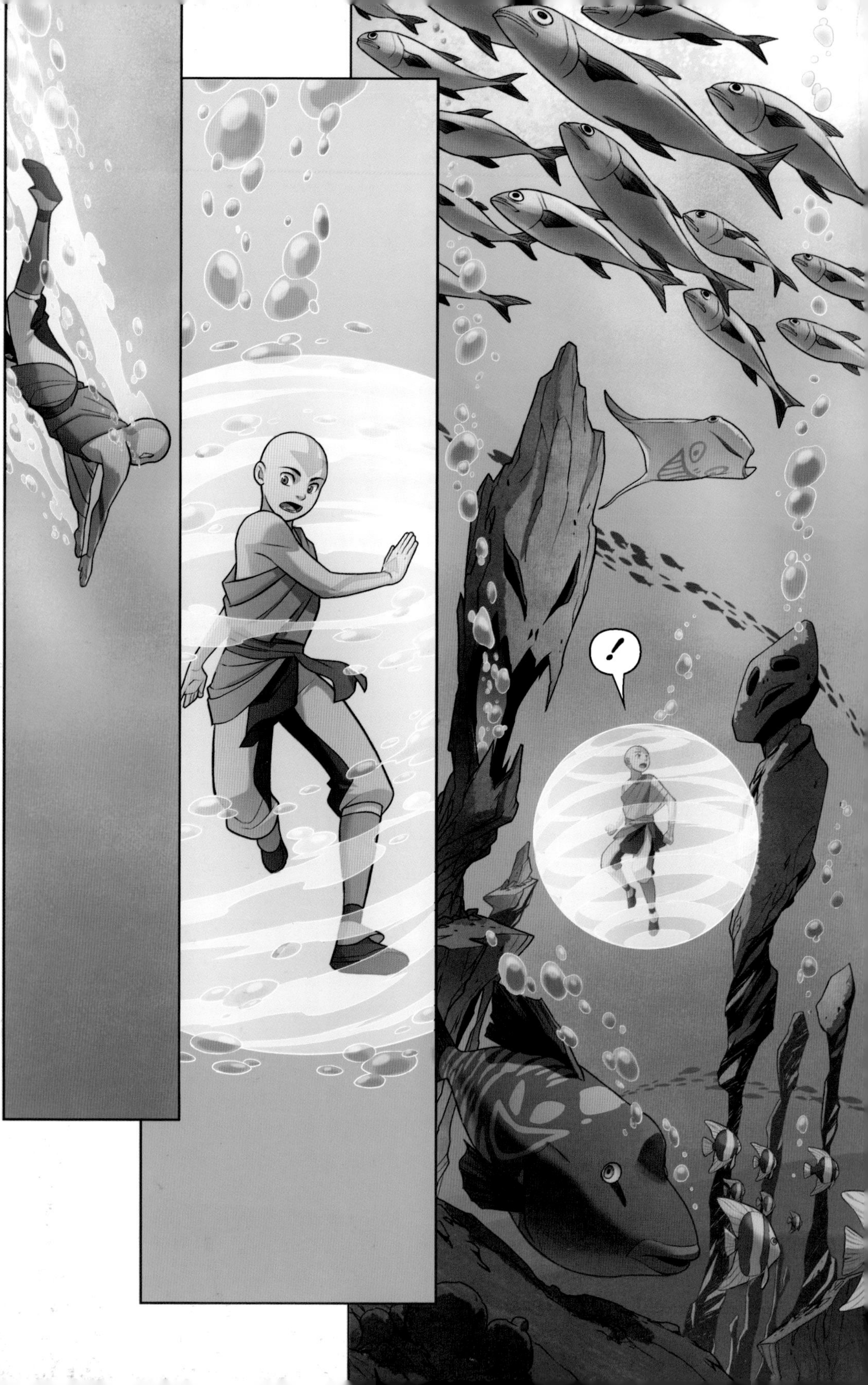
!

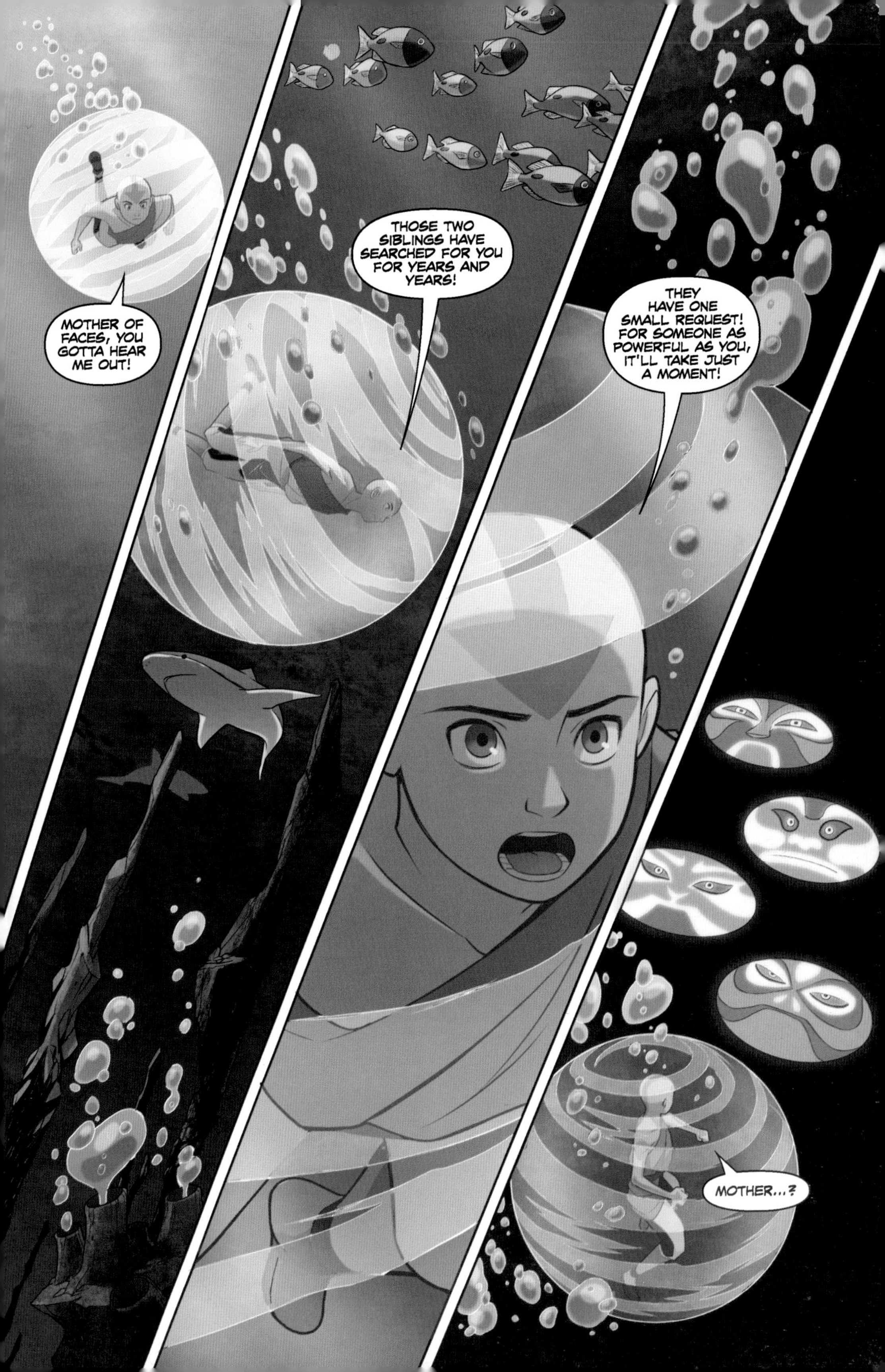
MOTHER OF FACES, YOU GOTTA HEAR ME OUT!
THOSE TWO SIBLINGS HAVE SEARCHED FOR YOU FOR YEARS AND YEARS!
THEY HAVE ONE SMALL REQUEST! FOR SOMEONE AS POWERFUL AS YOU, IT'LL TAKE JUST A MOMENT!
MOTHER...?

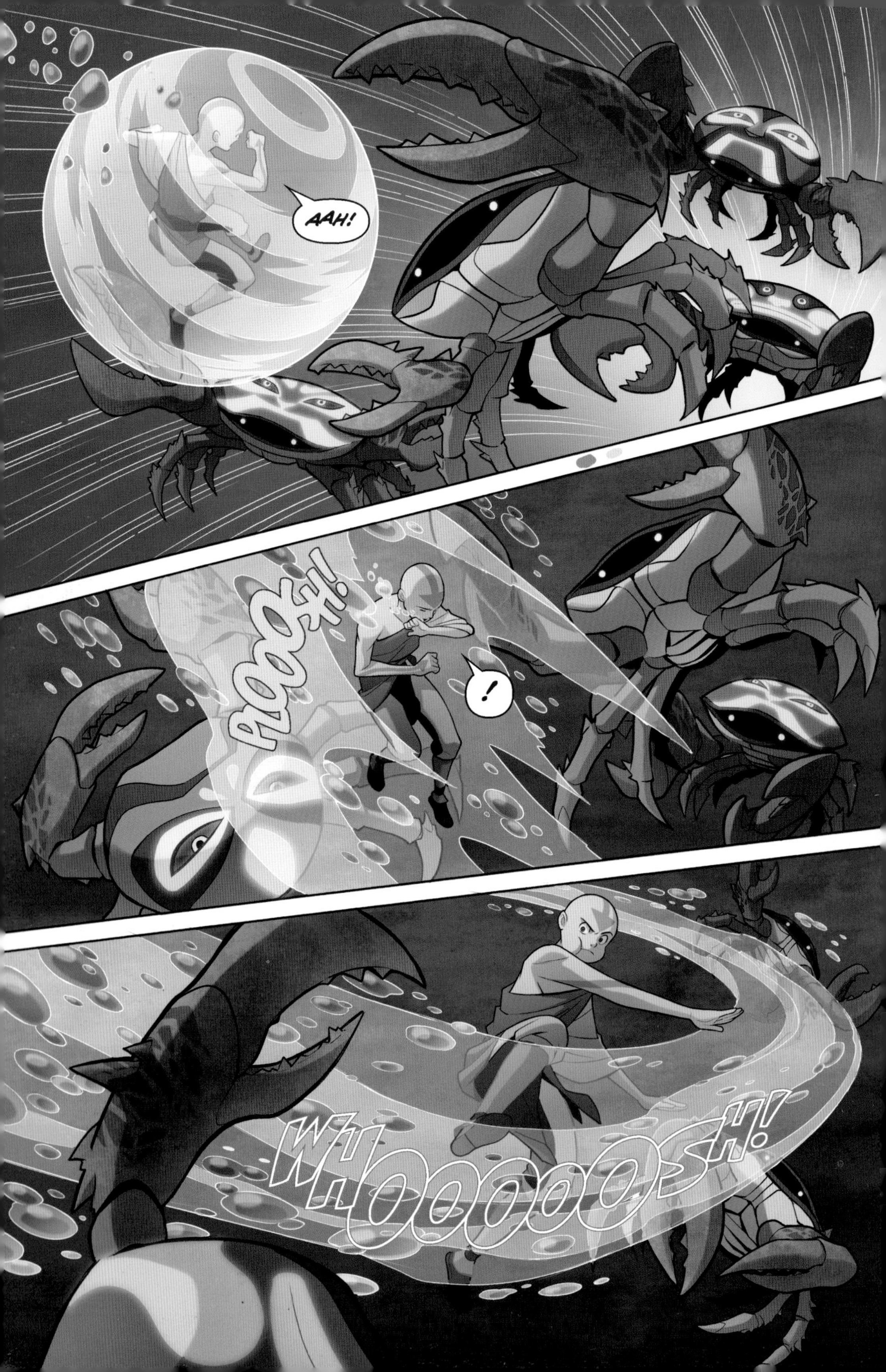
AAH!
FLOOSH!
!
WHOOOOOOSH!

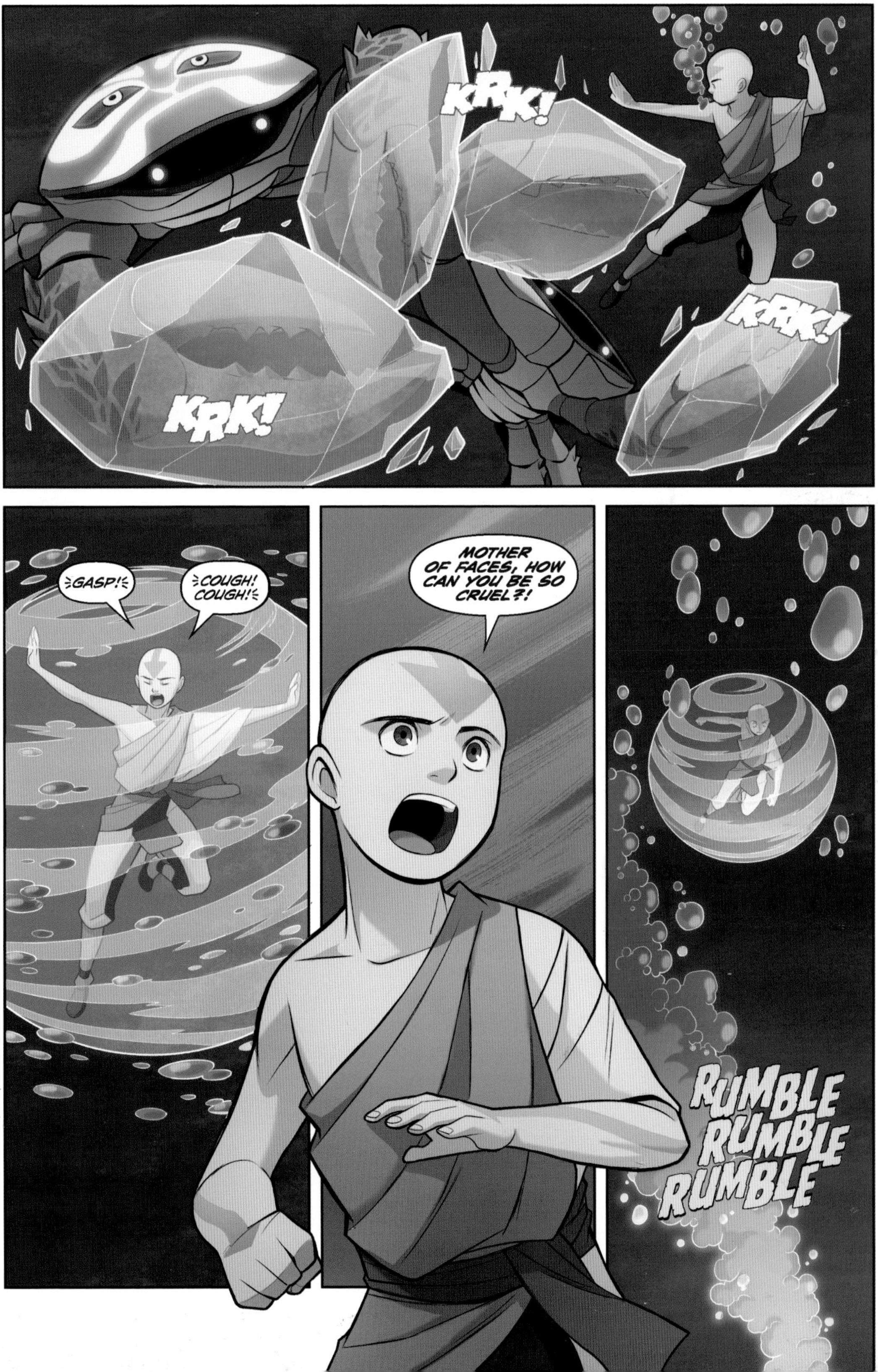
KRK!
KRK!
KRK!
GASP!
COUGH! COUGH!
MOTHER OF FACES, HOW CAN YOU BE SO CRUEL?!
RUMBLE RUMBLE RUMBLE

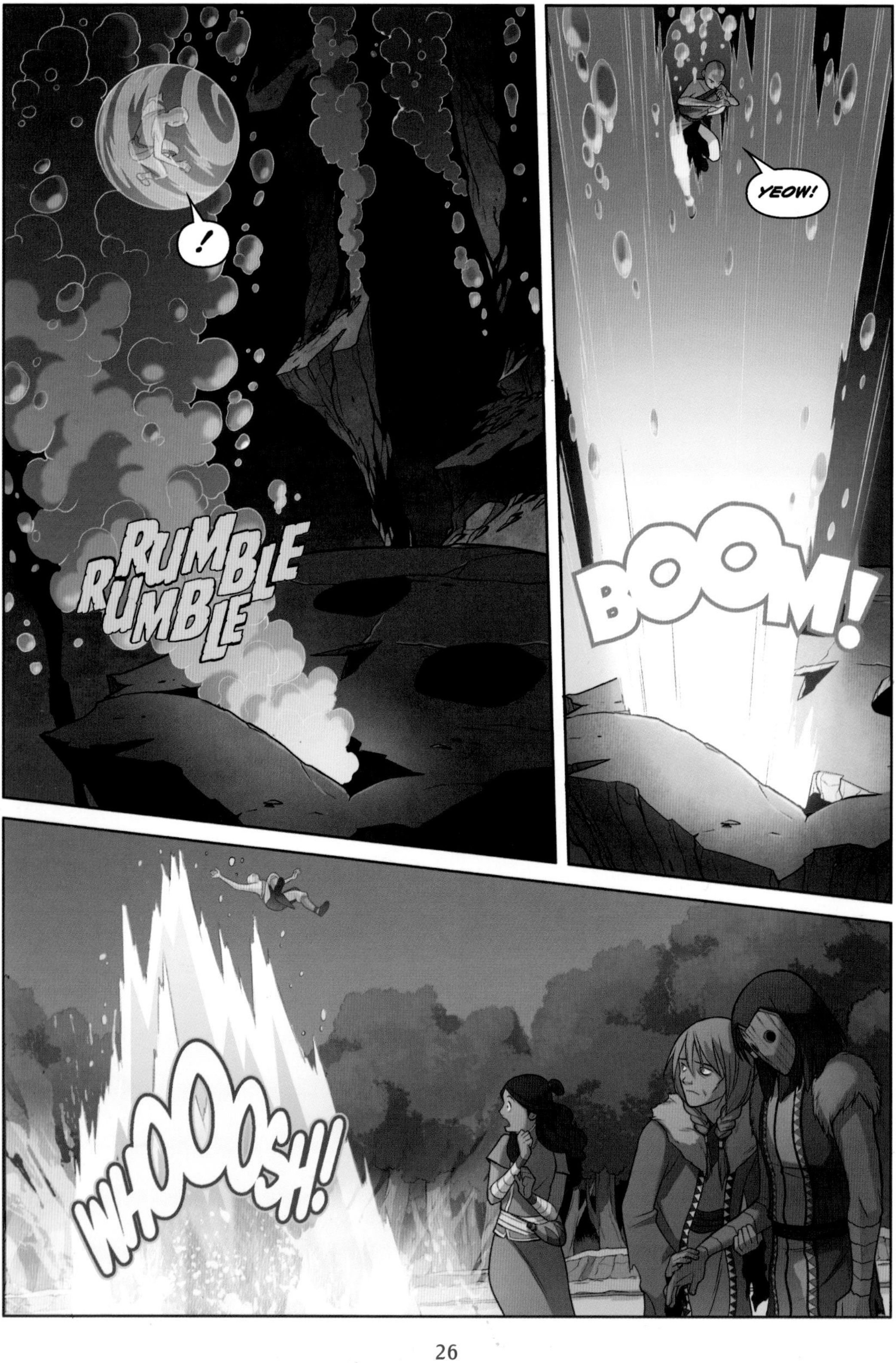
!
RUMBLE RUMBLE
YEOW!
BOOM!
WHOOOSH!

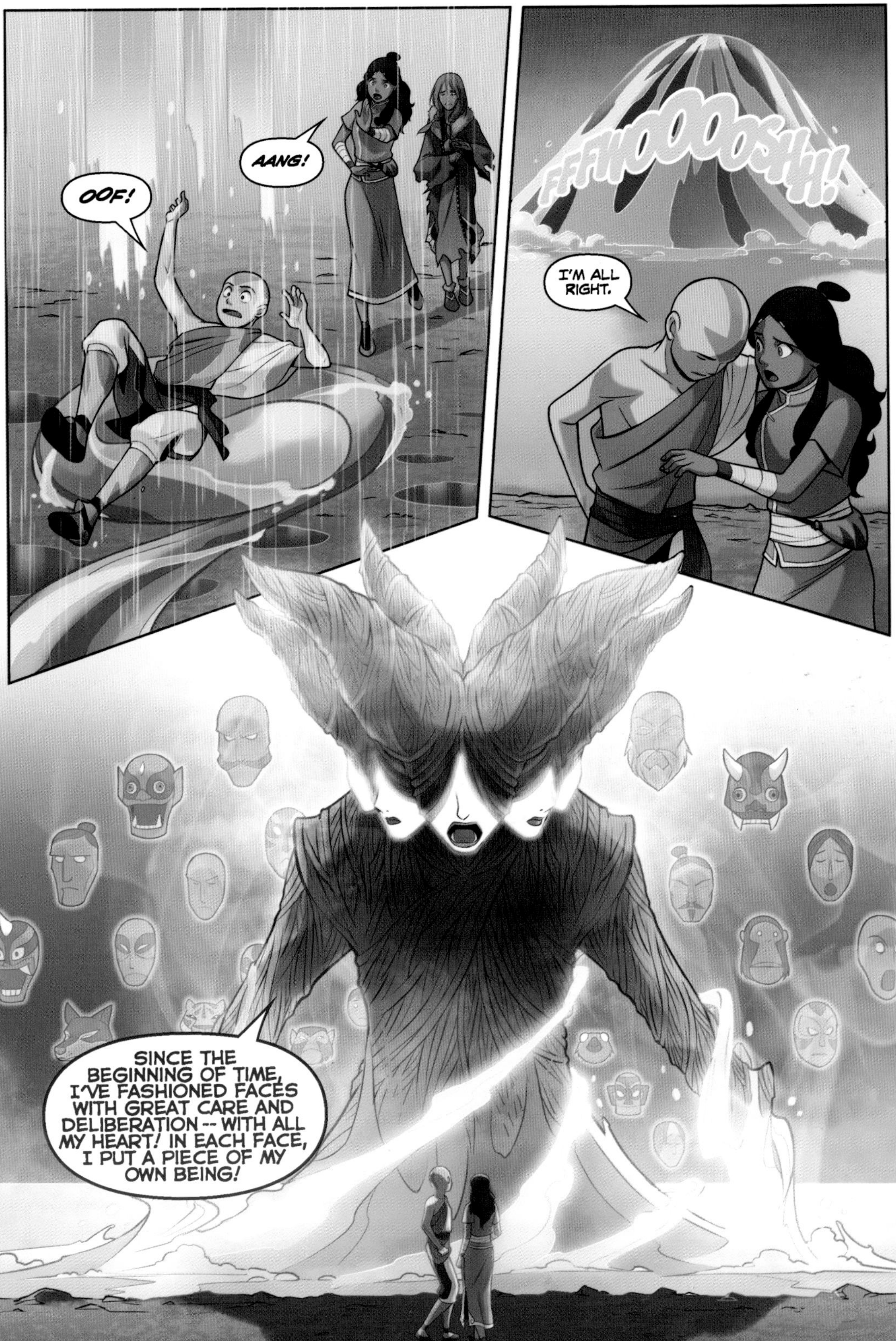
OOF!
AANG!
FFFWOOOOOSHH!
I'M ALL RIGHT.
SINCE THE BEGINNING OF TIME, I'VE FASHIONED FACES WITH GREAT CARE AND DELIBERATION -- WITH ALL MY HEART! IN EACH FACE, I PUT A PIECE OF MY OWN BEING!

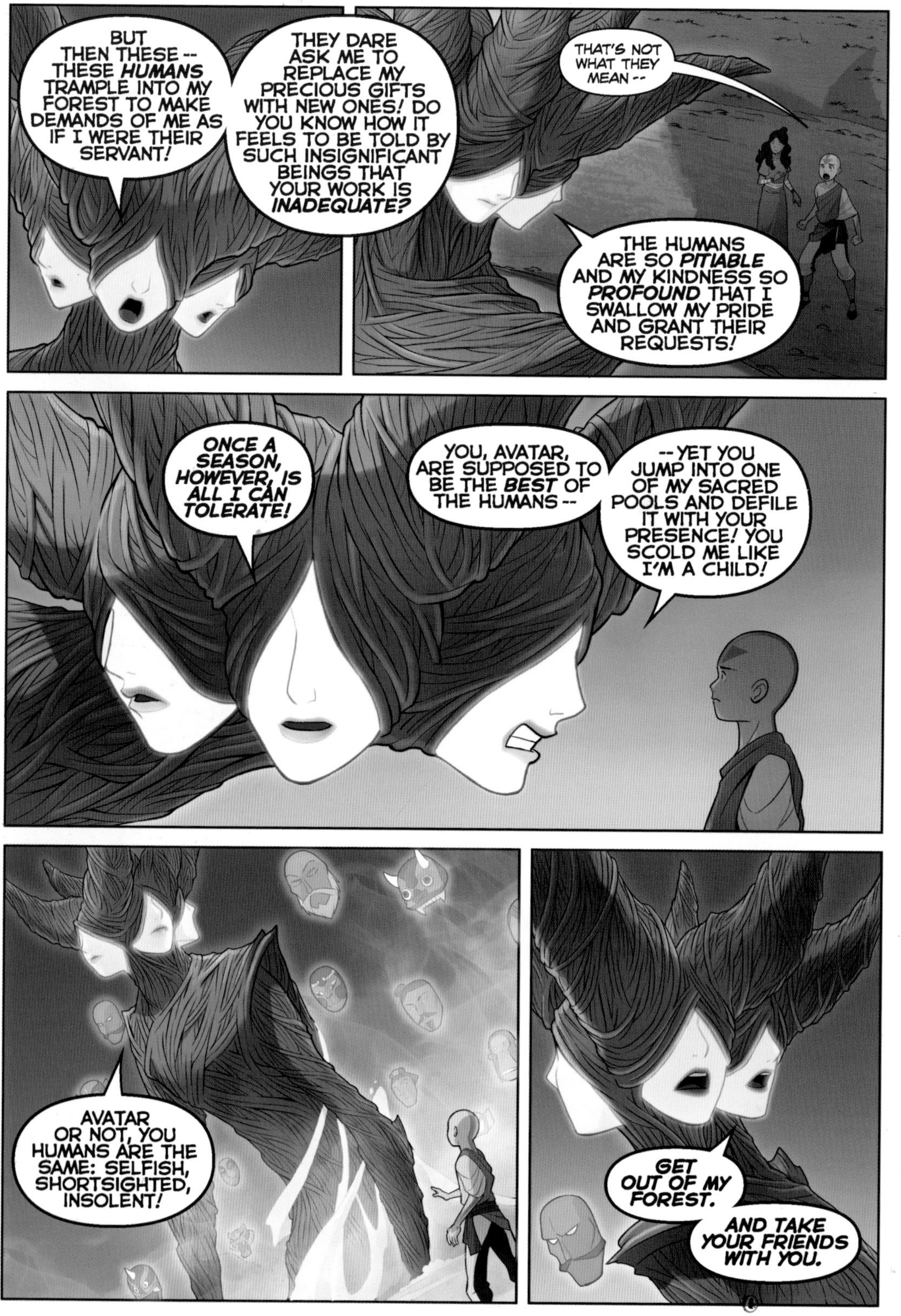
BUT THEN THESE -- THESE HUMANS TRAMPLE INTO MY FOREST TO MAKE DEMANDS OF ME AS IF I WERE THEIR SERVANT!
THEY DARE ASK ME TO REPLACE MY PRECIOUS GIFTS WITH NEW ONES! DO YOU KNOW HOW IT FEELS TO BE TOLD BY SUCH INSIGNIFICANT BEINGS THAT YOUR WORK IS INADEQUATE?
THAT'S NOT WHAT THEY MEAN --
THE HUMANS ARE SO PITIABLE AND MY KINDNESS SO PROFOUND THAT I SWALLOW MY PRIDE AND GRANT THEIR REQUESTS!
ONCE A SEASON, HOWEVER, IS ALL I CAN TOLERATE!
YOU, AVATAR, ARE SUPPOSED TO BE THE BEST OF THE HUMANS --
-- YET YOU JUMP INTO ONE OF MY SACRED POOLS AND DEFILE IT WITH YOUR PRESENCE! YOU SCOLD ME LIKE I'M A CHILD!
AVATAR OR NOT, YOU HUMANS ARE THE SAME: SELFISH, SHORTSIGHTED, INSOLENT!
GET OUT OF MY FOREST.
AND TAKE YOUR FRIENDS WITH YOU.

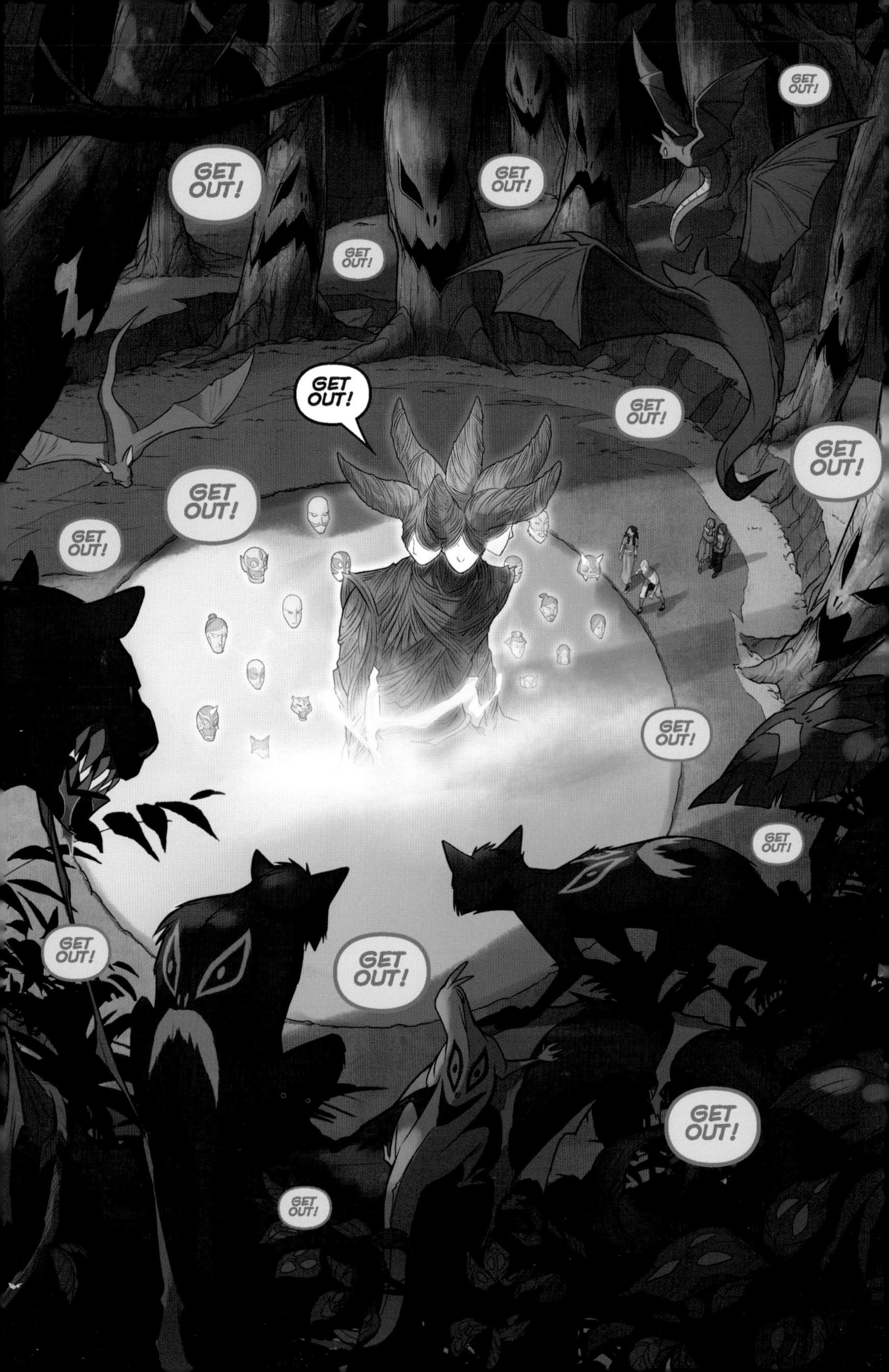
GET OUT!
GET OUT!
GET OUT!
GET OUT!
GET OUT!
GET OUT!
GET OUT!
GET OUT!
GET OUT!
GET OUT!
GET OUT!
GET OUT!
GET OUT!
GET OUT!
GET OUT!

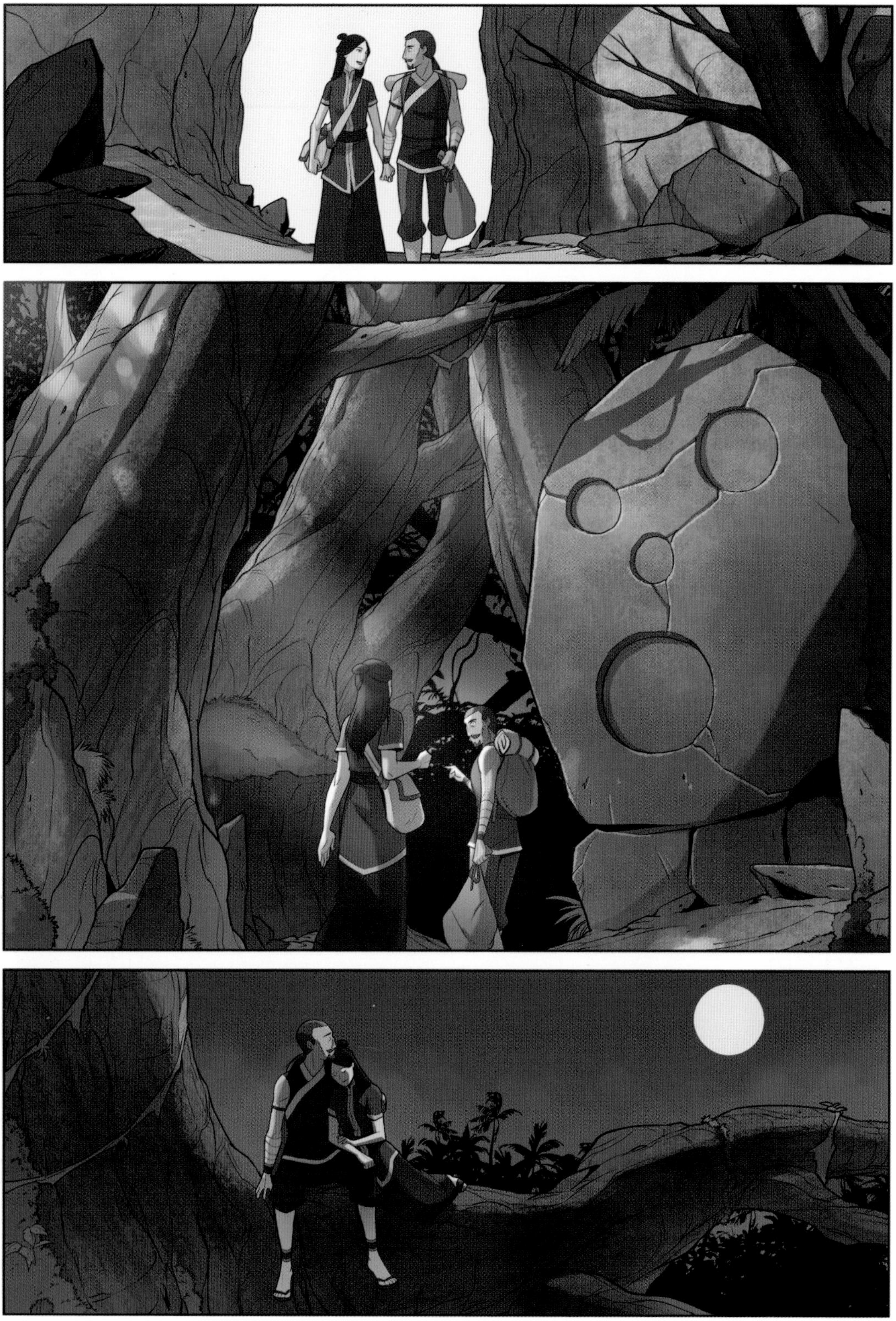

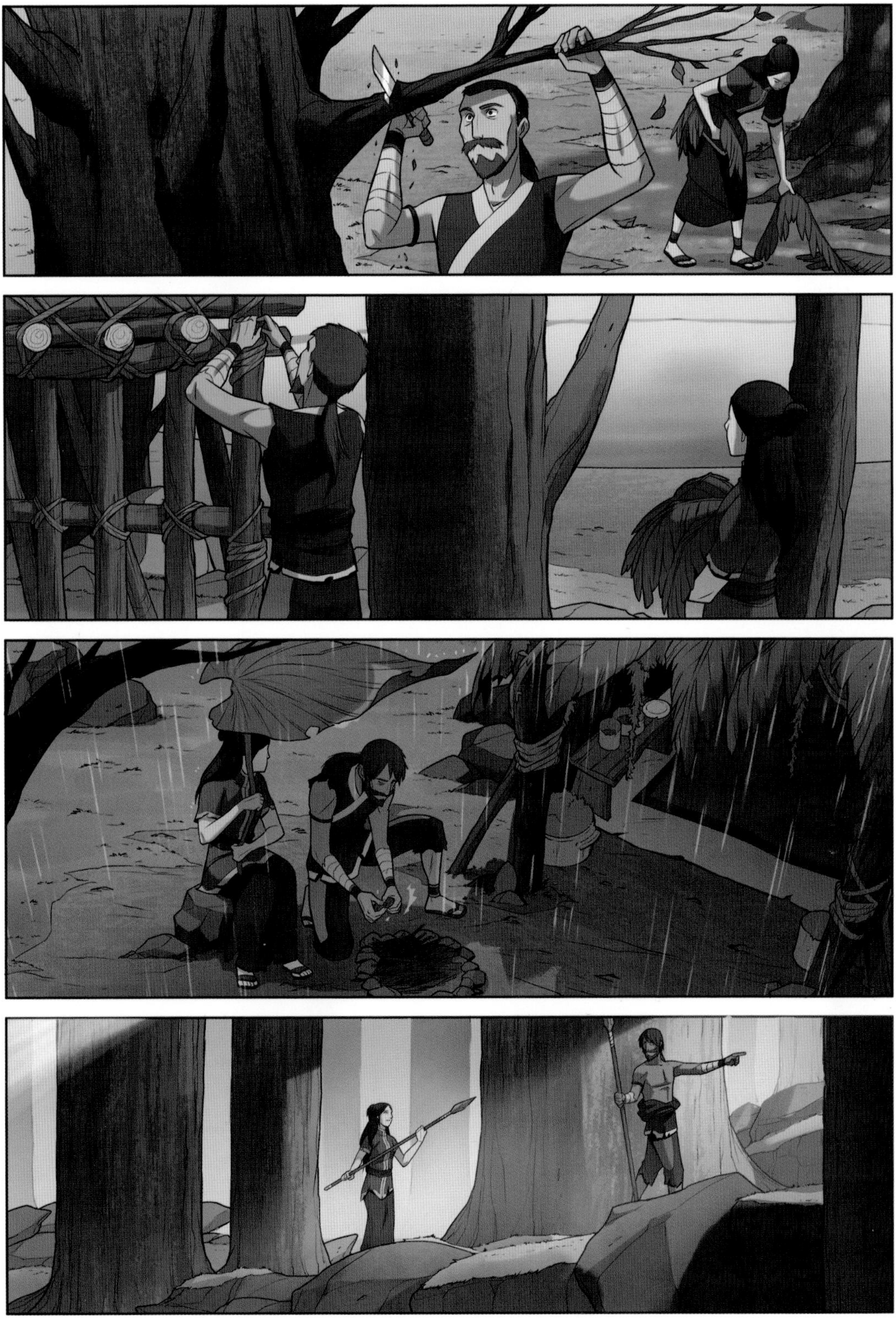

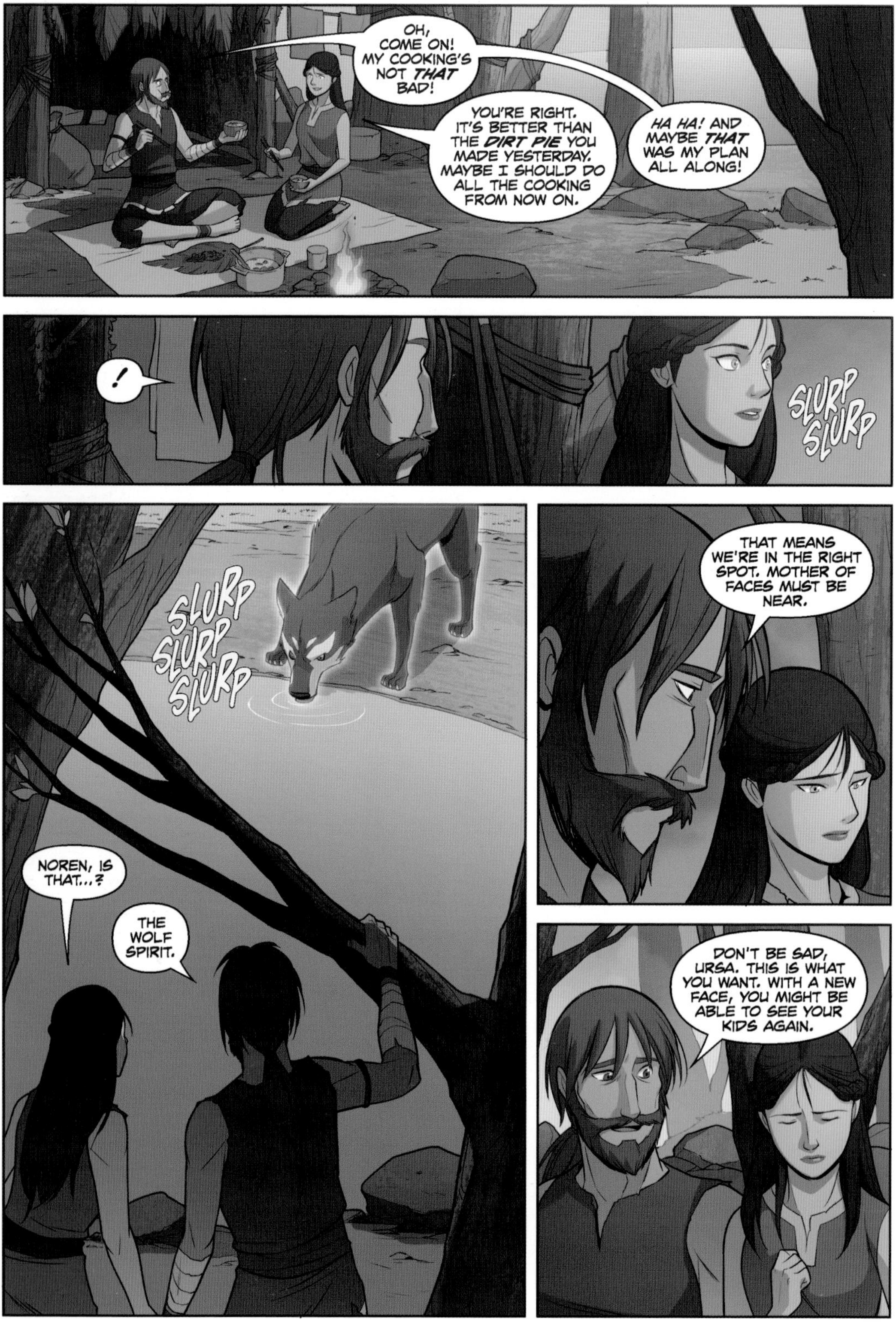
OH, COME ON! MY COOKING'S NOT *THAT* BAD!
YOU'RE RIGHT. IT'S BETTER THAN THE *DIRT PIE* YOU MADE YESTERDAY. MAYBE I SHOULD DO ALL THE COOKING FROM NOW ON.
*HA HA!* AND MAYBE *THAT* WAS MY PLAN ALL ALONG!
!
SLURP SLURP
SLURP SLURP SLURP
NOREN, IS THAT...?
THE WOLF SPIRIT.
THAT MEANS WE'RE IN THE RIGHT SPOT. MOTHER OF FACES MUST BE NEAR.
DON'T BE SAD, URSA. THIS IS WHAT YOU WANT. WITH A NEW FACE, YOU MIGHT BE ABLE TO SEE YOUR KIDS AGAIN.

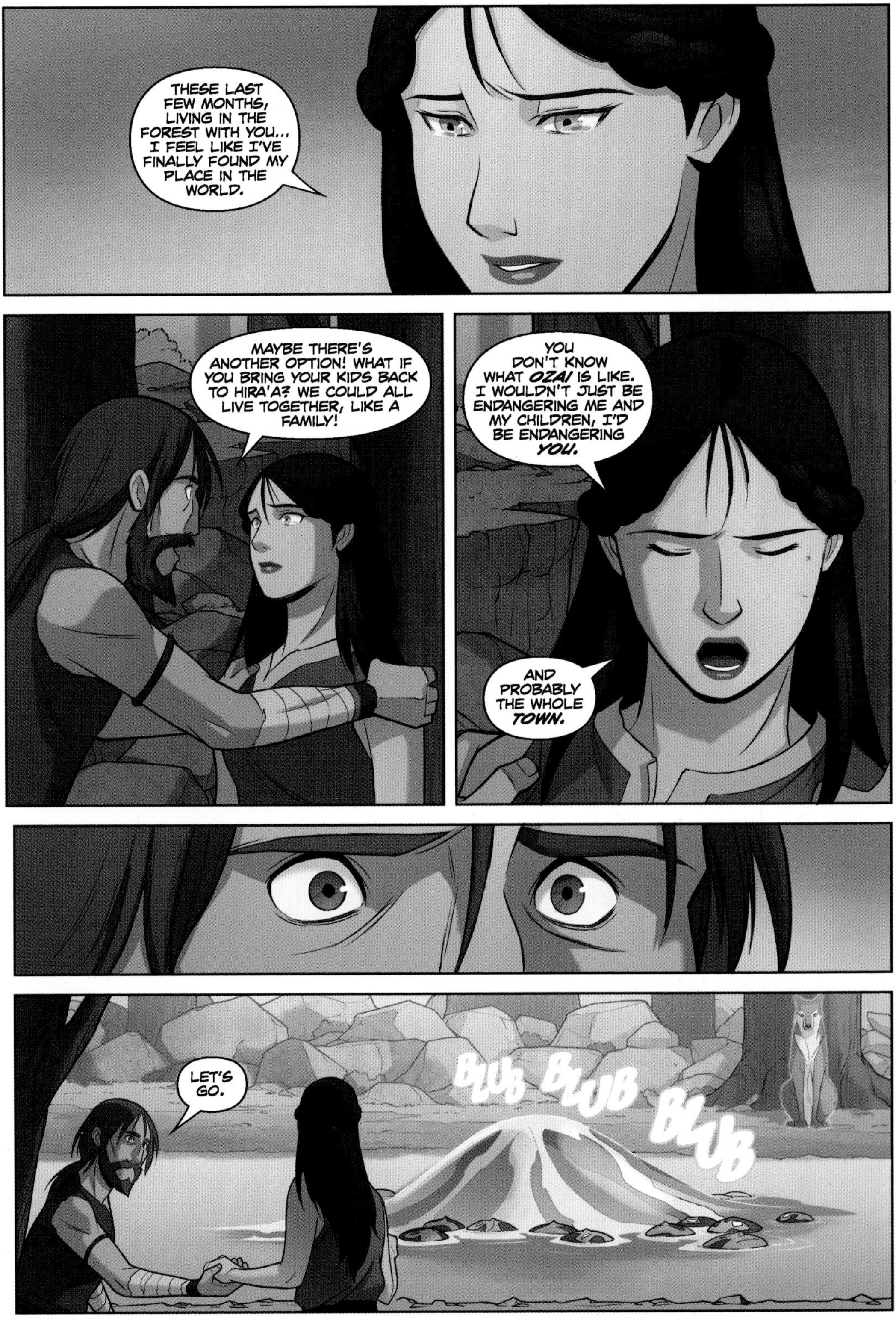
THESE LAST FEW MONTHS, LIVING IN THE FOREST WITH YOU... I FEEL LIKE I'VE FINALLY FOUND MY PLACE IN THE WORLD.
MAYBE THERE'S ANOTHER OPTION! WHAT IF YOU BRING YOUR KIDS BACK TO HIRA'A? WE COULD ALL LIVE TOGETHER, LIKE A FAMILY!
YOU DON'T KNOW WHAT OZAI IS LIKE. I WOULDN'T JUST BE ENDANGERING ME AND MY CHILDREN, I'D BE ENDANGERING YOU.
AND PROBABLY THE WHOLE TOWN.
LET'S GO.
BLUB BLUB BLUB

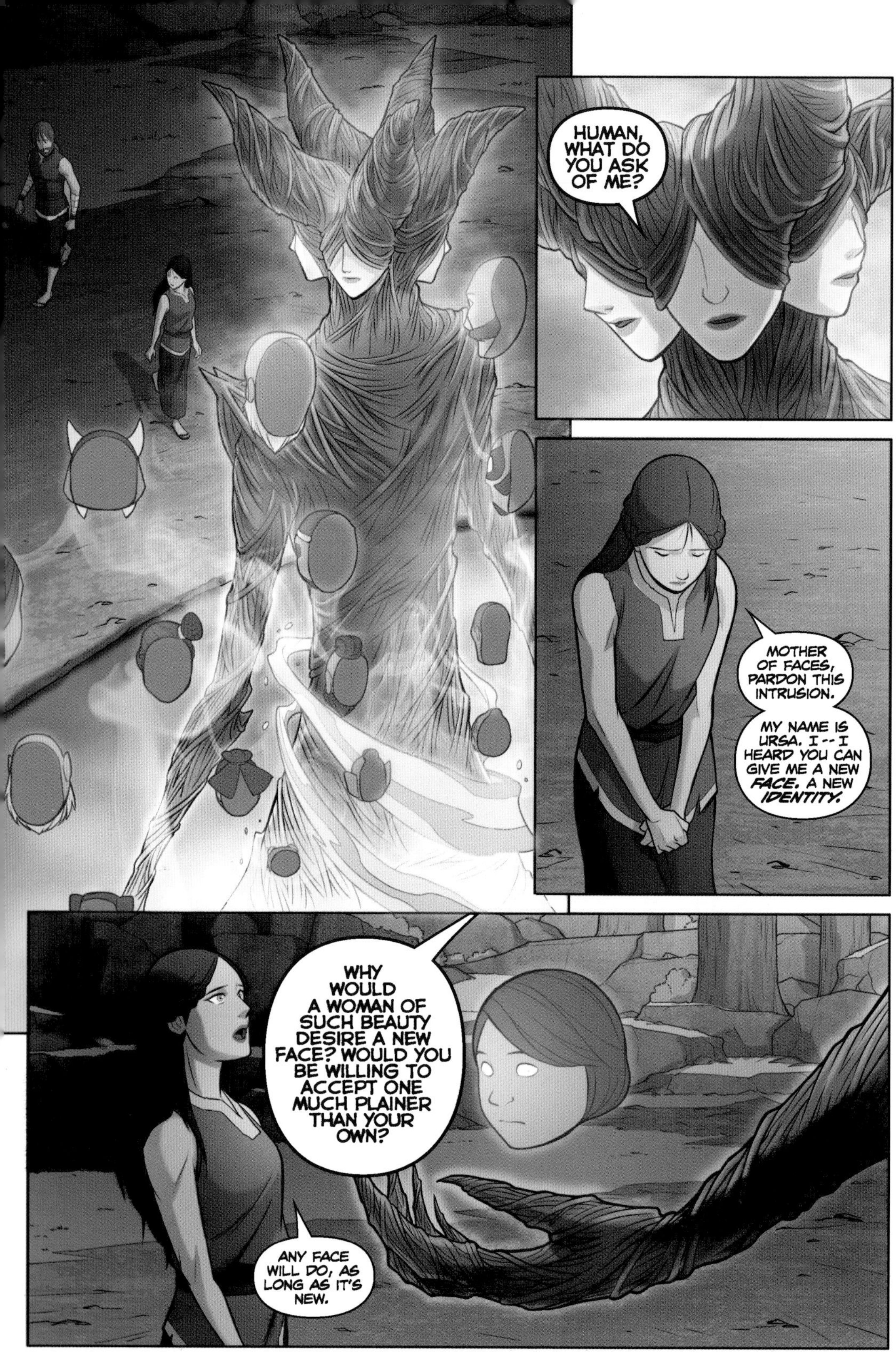
HUMAN, WHAT DO YOU ASK OF ME?
MOTHER OF FACES, PARDON THIS INTRUSION.
MY NAME IS URSA. I -- I HEARD YOU CAN GIVE ME A NEW *FACE.* A NEW *IDENTITY.*
WHY WOULD A WOMAN OF SUCH BEAUTY DESIRE A NEW FACE? WOULD YOU BE WILLING TO ACCEPT ONE MUCH PLAINER THAN YOUR OWN?
ANY FACE WILL DO, AS LONG AS IT'S NEW.

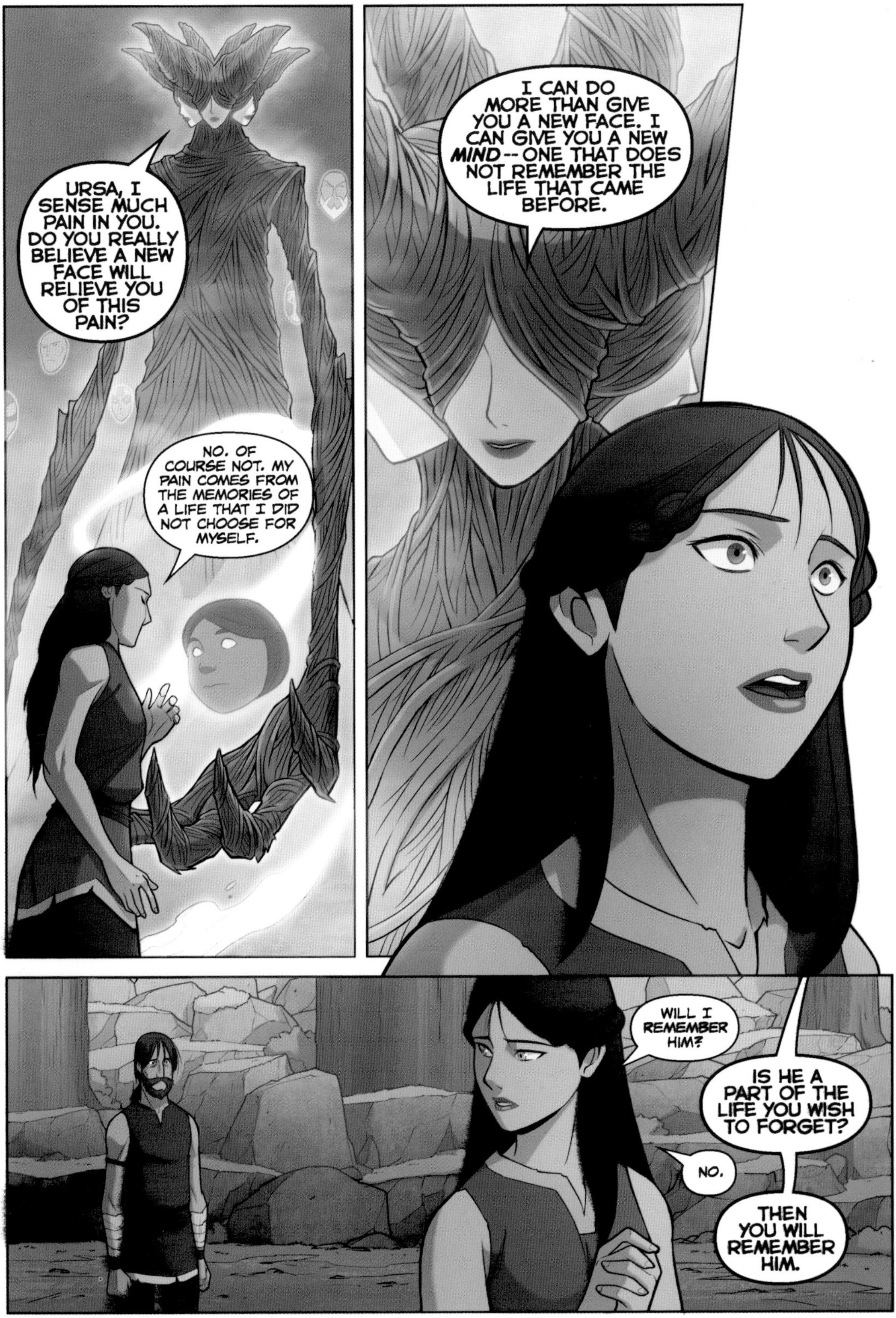
URSA, I SENSE MUCH PAIN IN YOU. DO YOU REALLY BELIEVE A NEW FACE WILL RELIEVE YOU OF THIS PAIN?
NO. OF COURSE NOT. MY PAIN COMES FROM THE MEMORIES OF A LIFE THAT I DID NOT CHOOSE FOR MYSELF.
I CAN DO MORE THAN GIVE YOU A NEW FACE. I CAN GIVE YOU A NEW *MIND*-- ONE THAT DOES NOT REMEMBER THE LIFE THAT CAME BEFORE.
WILL I REMEMBER HIM?
IS HE A PART OF THE LIFE YOU WISH TO FORGET?
NO.
THEN YOU WILL REMEMBER HIM.

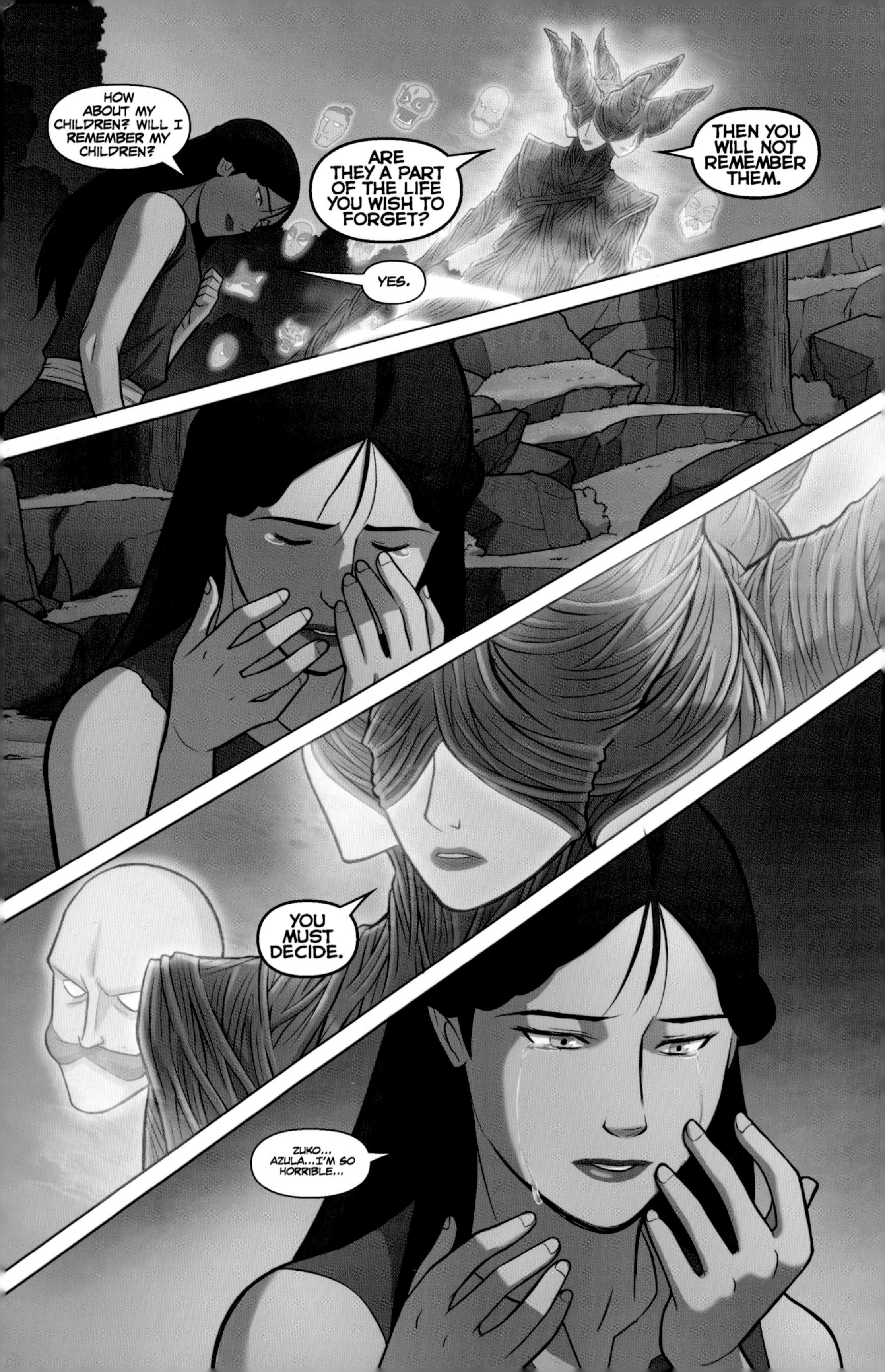
HOW ABOUT MY CHILDREN? WILL I REMEMBER MY CHILDREN?
ARE THEY A PART OF THE LIFE YOU WISH TO FORGET?
YES.
THEN YOU WILL NOT REMEMBER THEM.
YOU MUST DECIDE.
ZUKO... AZULA... I'M SO HORRIBLE...

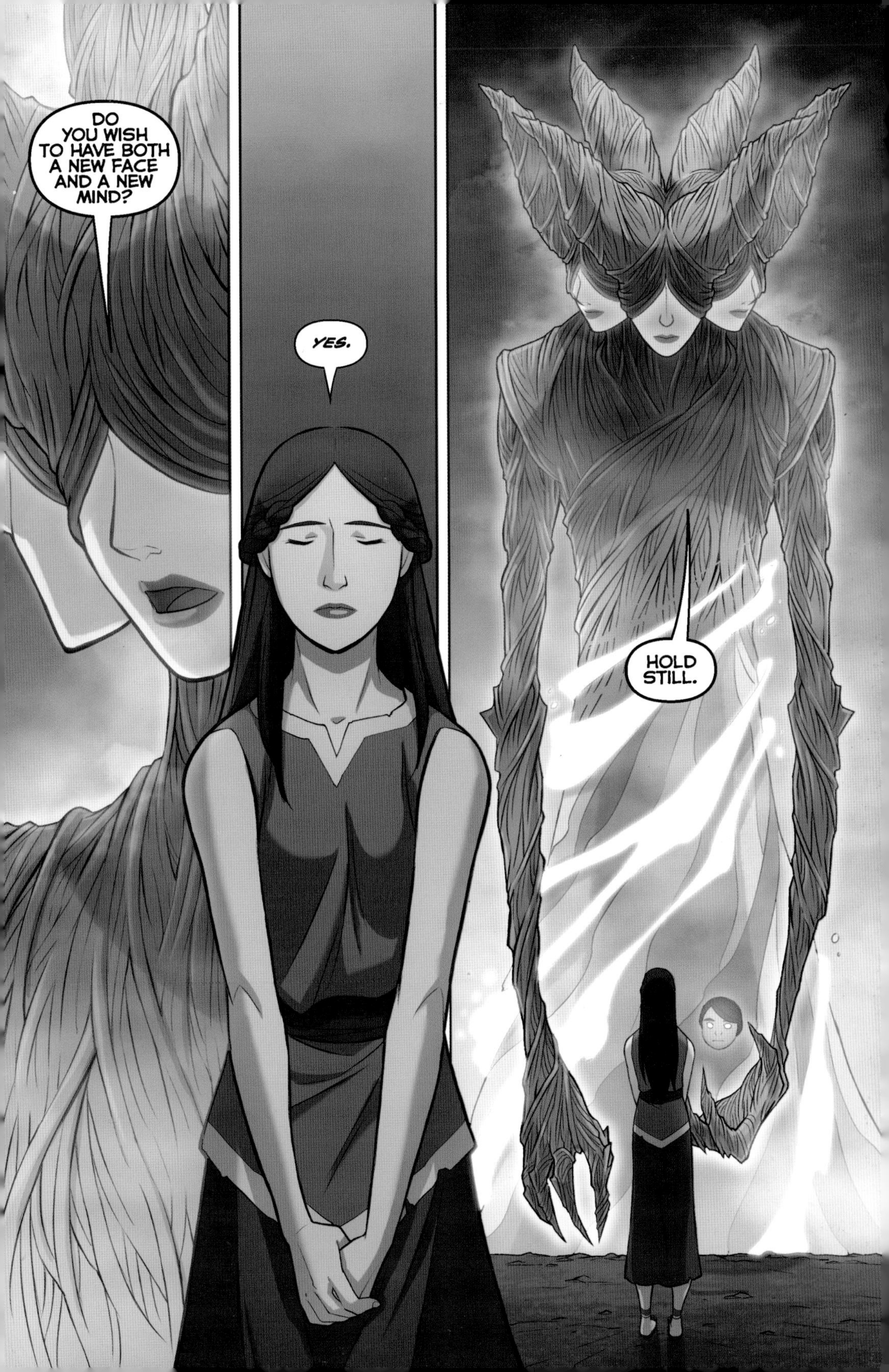
DO YOU WISH TO HAVE BOTH A NEW FACE AND A NEW MIND?
YES.
HOLD STILL.

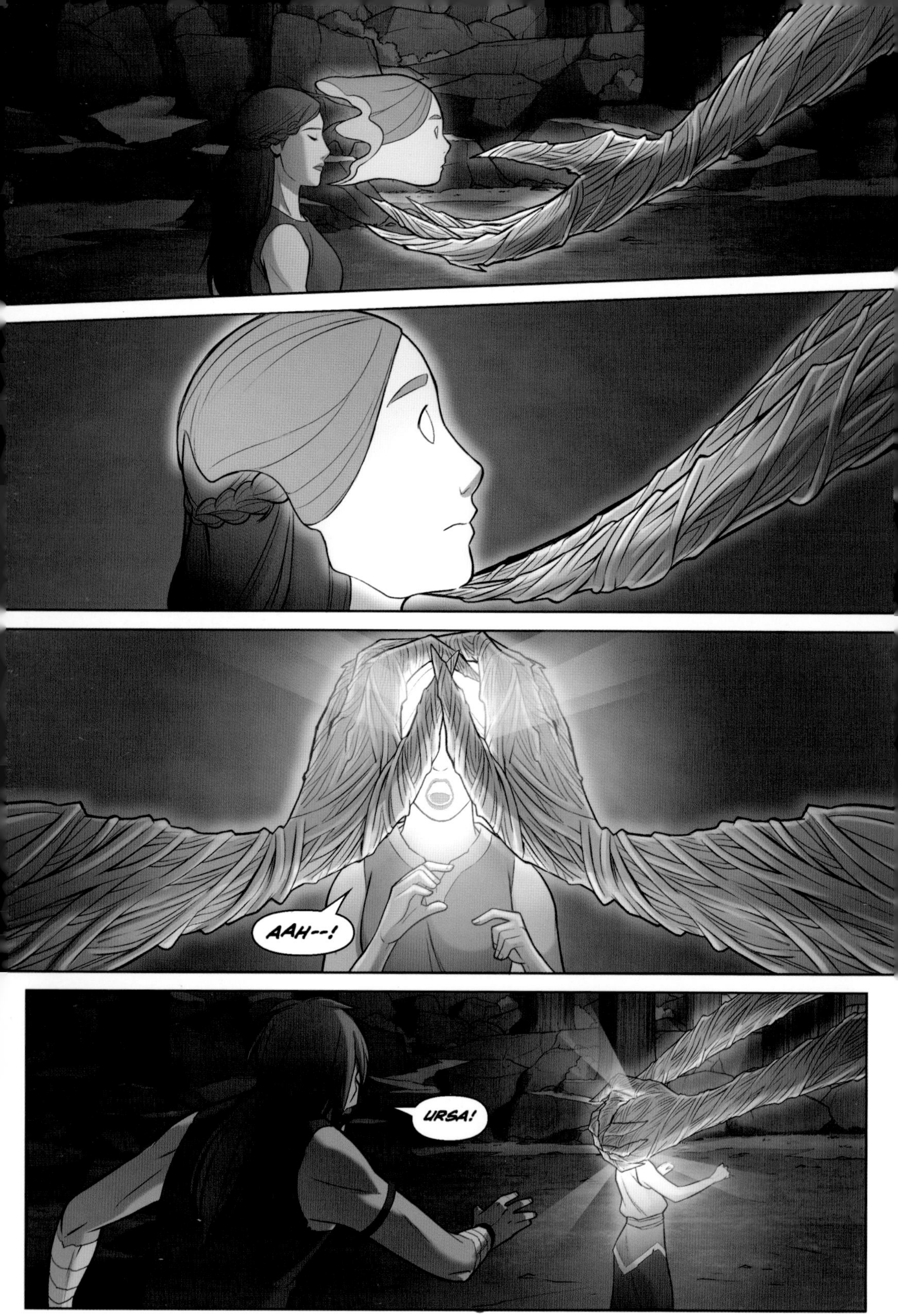
AAH--!
URSA!

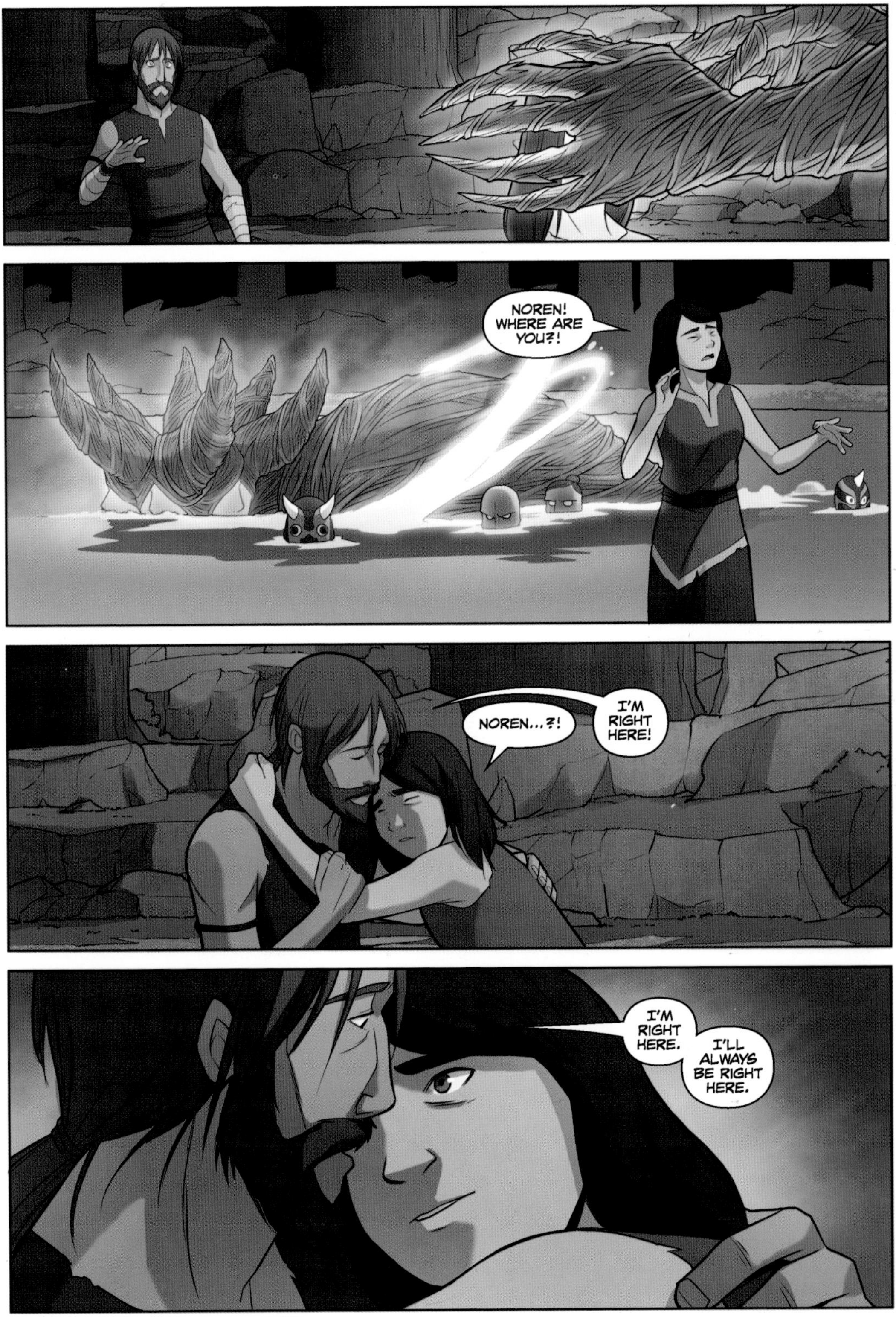
NOREN! WHERE ARE YOU?!
NOREN...?!
I'M RIGHT HERE!
I'M RIGHT HERE.
I'LL ALWAYS BE RIGHT HERE.

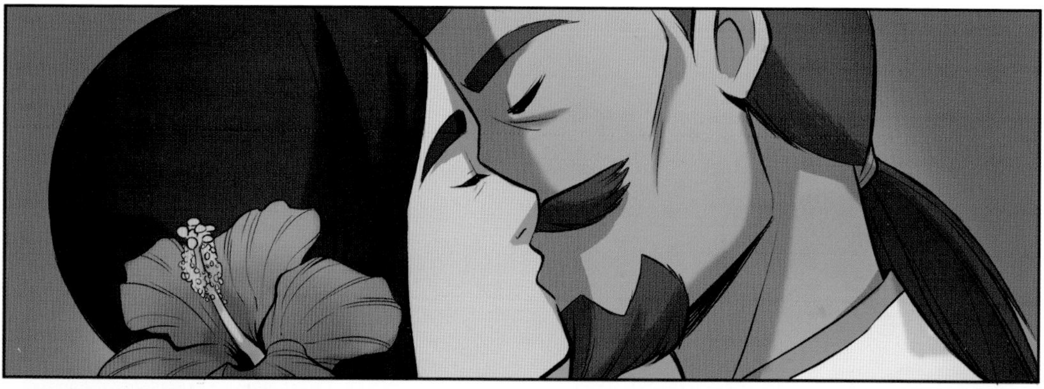

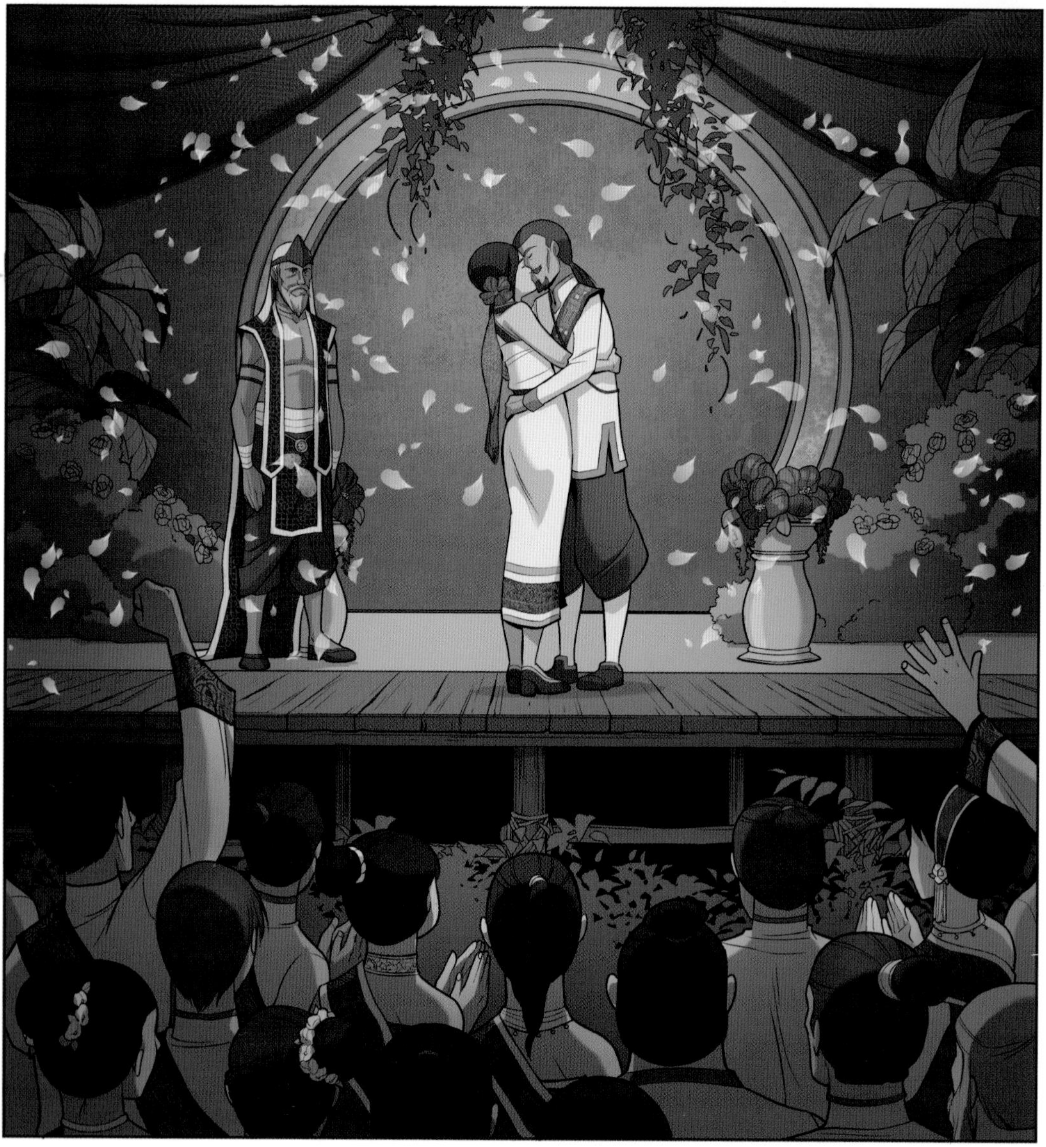

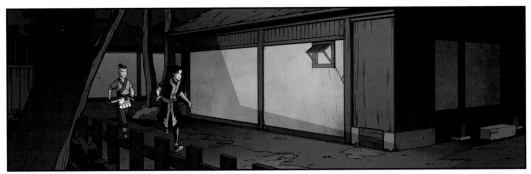

IT'S SO QUIET.

TOO QUIET.

ZUKO, WHAT'S GOING ON IN THERE? NOREN'S FAMILY...DON'T TELL ME AZULA--!

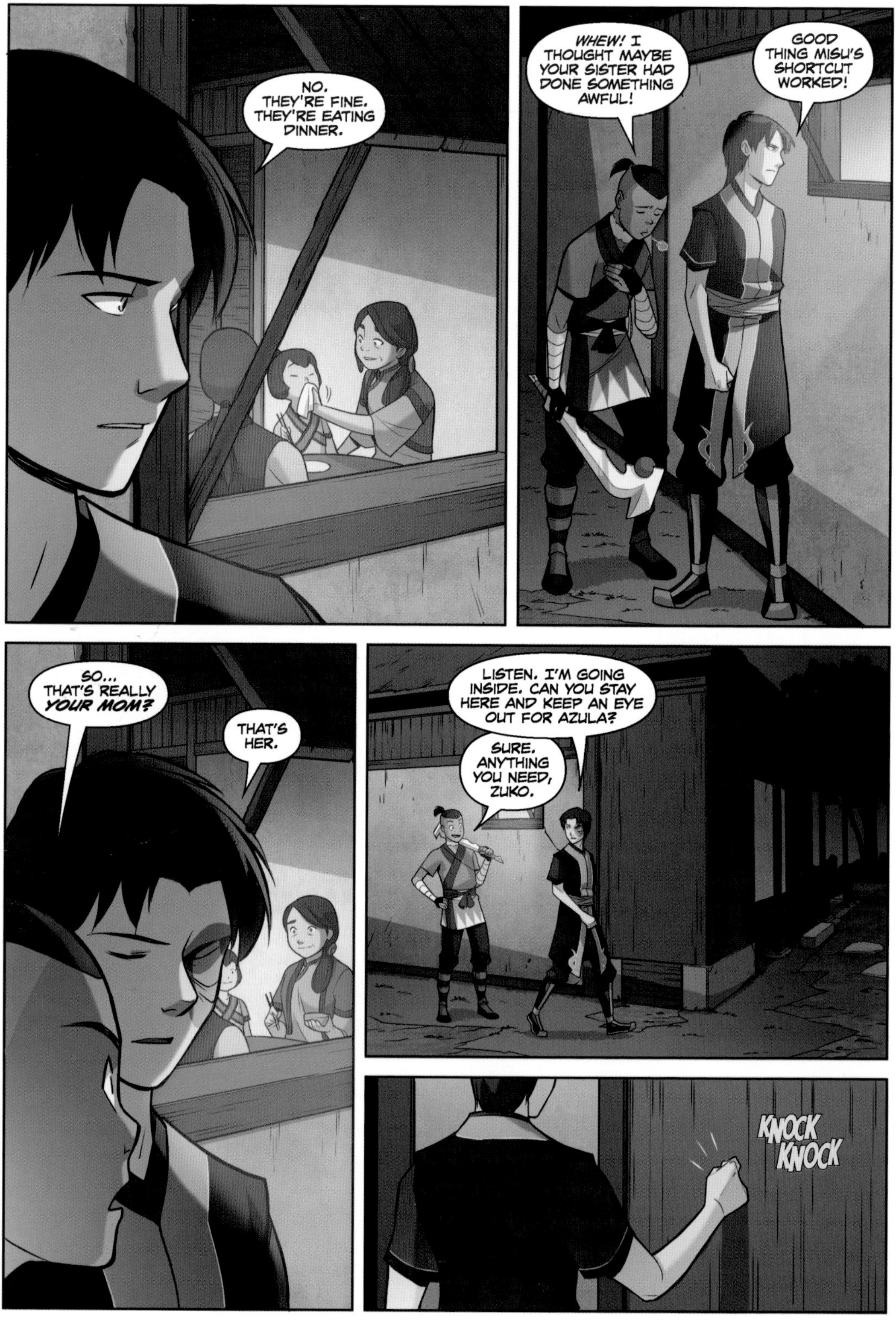
NO. THEY'RE FINE. THEY'RE EATING DINNER.
WHEW! I THOUGHT MAYBE YOUR SISTER HAD DONE SOMETHING AWFUL!
GOOD THING MISU'S SHORTCUT WORKED!
SO... THAT'S REALLY YOUR MOM?
THAT'S HER.
LISTEN. I'M GOING INSIDE. CAN YOU STAY HERE AND KEEP AN EYE OUT FOR AZULA?
SURE. ANYTHING YOU NEED, ZUKO.
KNOCK KNOCK

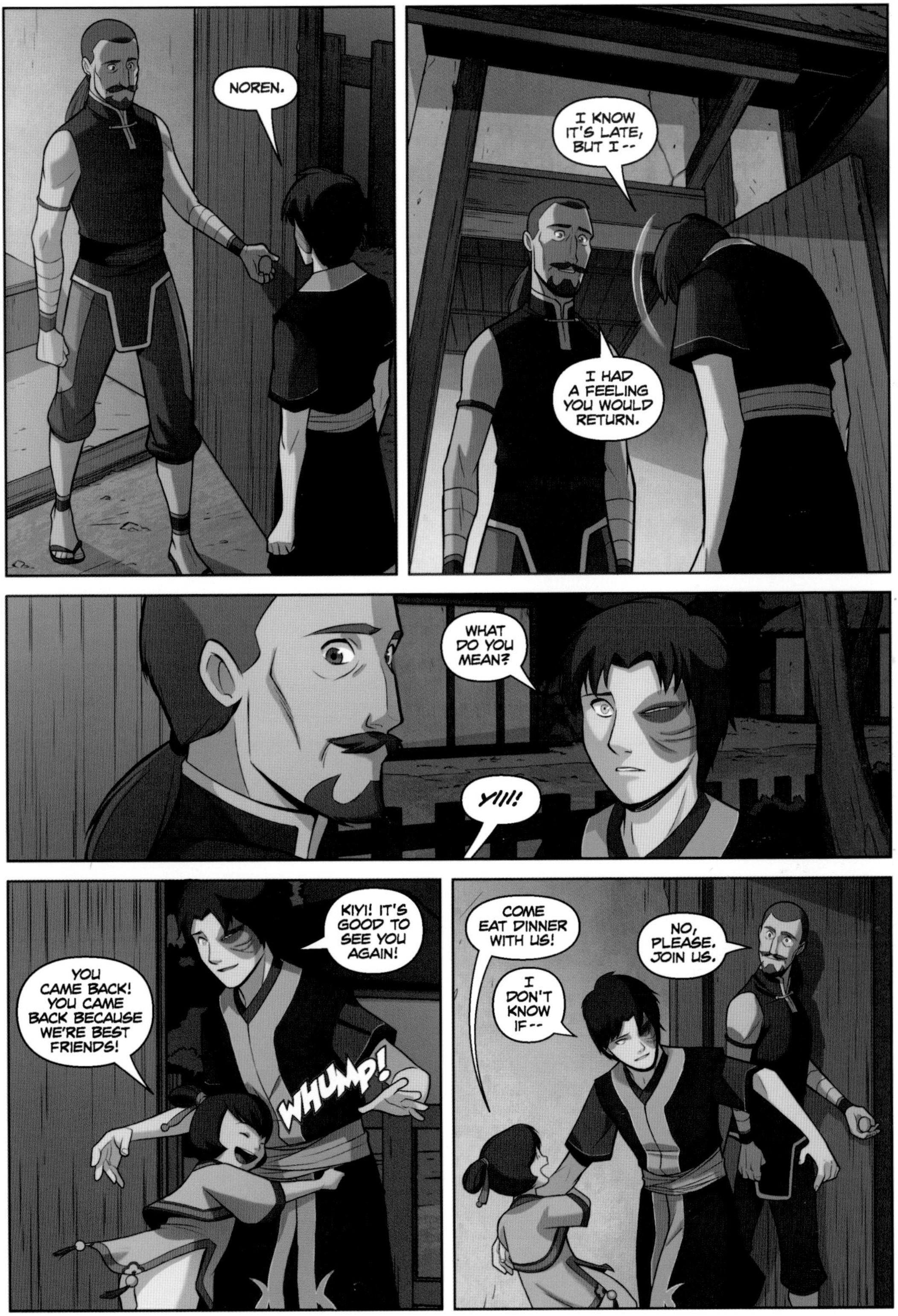
NOREN.
I KNOW IT'S LATE, BUT I --
I HAD A FEELING YOU WOULD RETURN.
WHAT DO YOU MEAN?
YIII!
KIYI! IT'S GOOD TO SEE YOU AGAIN!
YOU CAME BACK! YOU CAME BACK BECAUSE WE'RE BEST FRIENDS!
WHUMP!
COME EAT DINNER WITH US!
I DON'T KNOW IF --
NO, PLEASE. JOIN US.

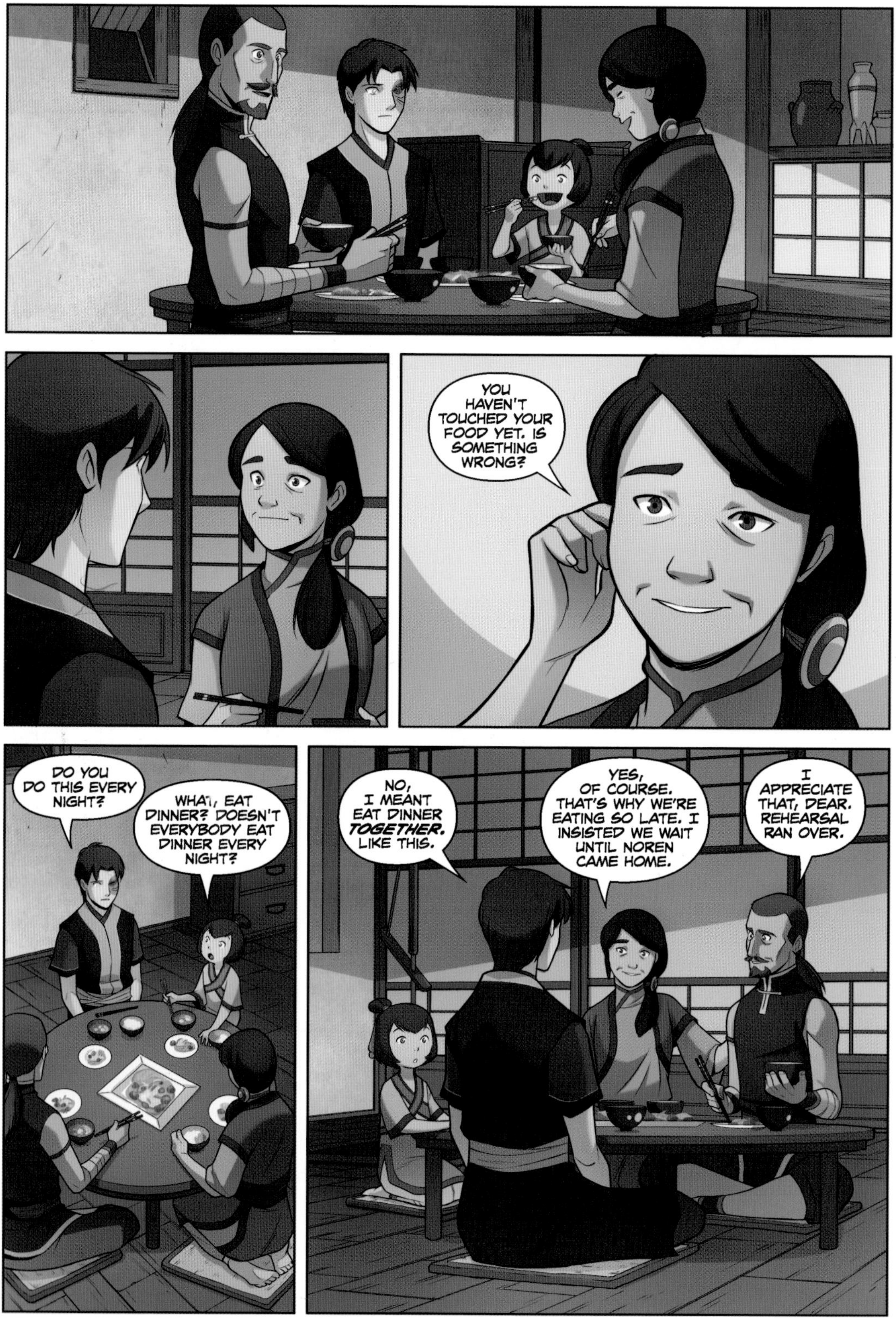
YOU HAVEN'T TOUCHED YOUR FOOD YET. IS SOMETHING WRONG?
DO YOU DO THIS EVERY NIGHT?
WHAT, EAT DINNER? DOESN'T EVERYBODY EAT DINNER EVERY NIGHT?
NO, I MEANT EAT DINNER *TOGETHER.* LIKE THIS.
YES, OF COURSE. THAT'S WHY WE'RE EATING SO LATE. I INSISTED WE WAIT UNTIL NOREN CAME HOME.
I APPRECIATE THAT, DEAR. REHEARSAL RAN OVER.

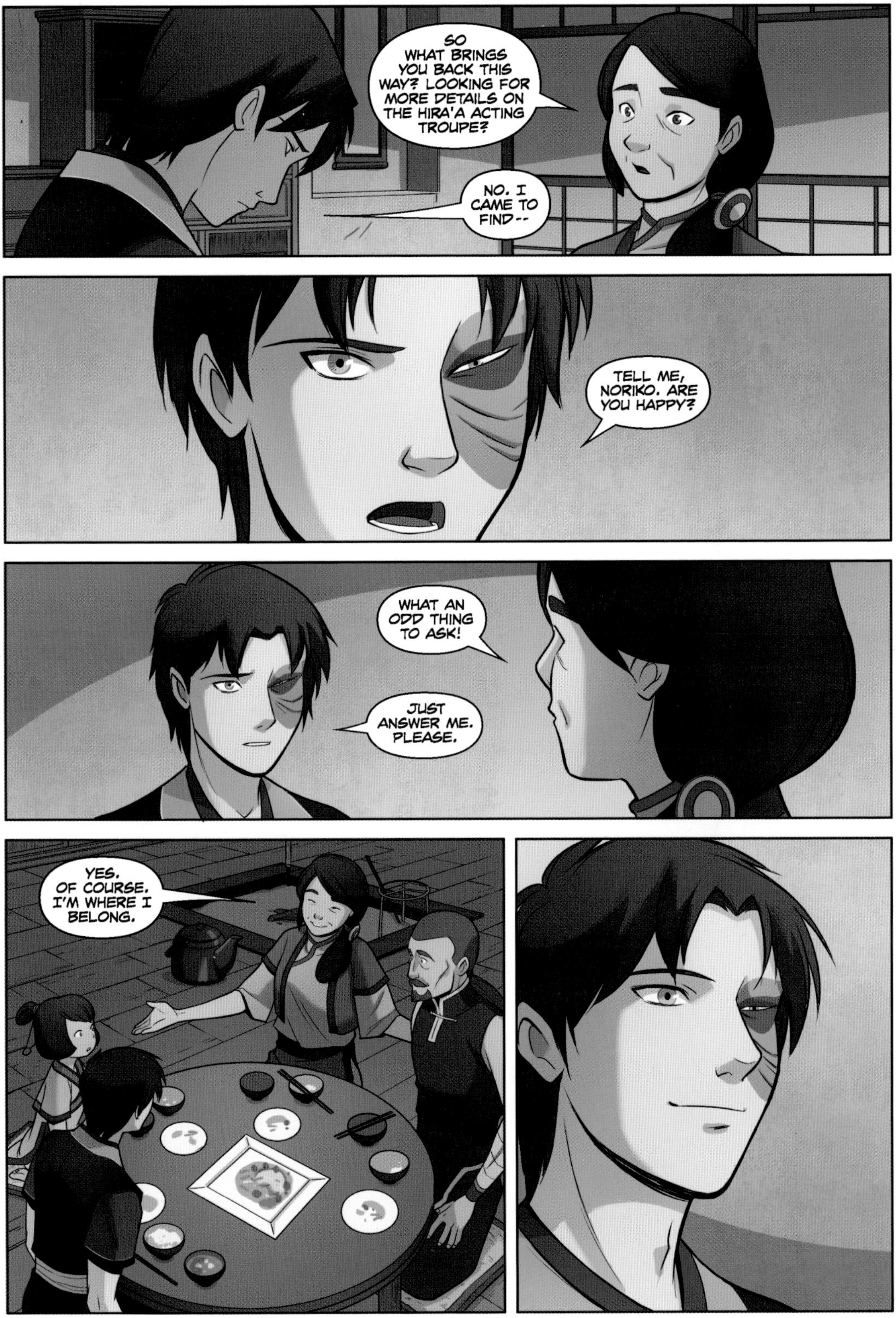
SO WHAT BRINGS YOU BACK THIS WAY? LOOKING FOR MORE DETAILS ON THE HIRA'A ACTING TROUPE?
NO. I CAME TO FIND--
TELL ME, NORIKO. ARE YOU HAPPY?
WHAT AN ODD THING TO ASK!
JUST ANSWER ME. PLEASE.
YES. OF COURSE. I'M WHERE I BELONG.

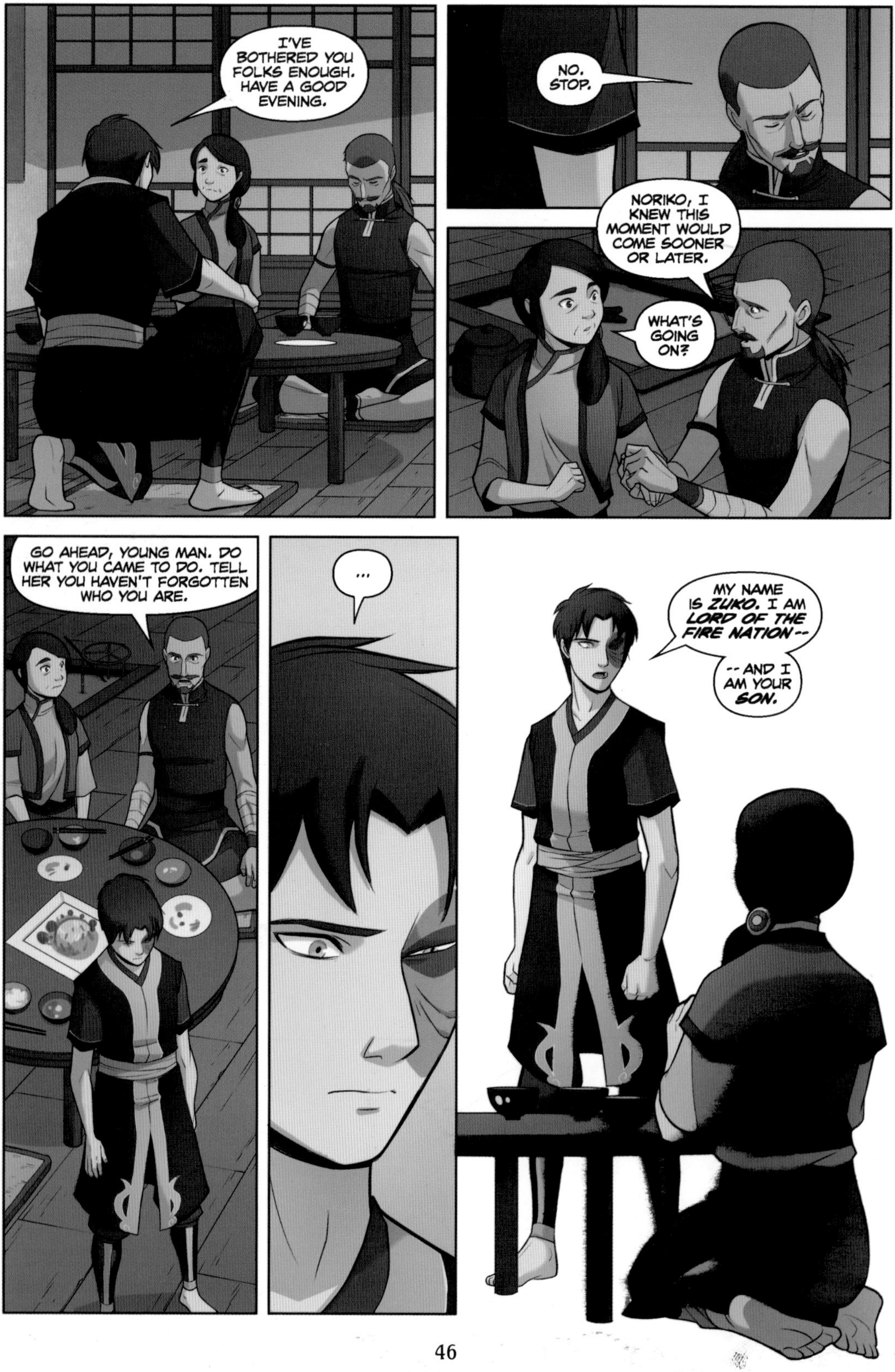
I'VE BOTHERED YOU FOLKS ENOUGH. HAVE A GOOD EVENING.
NO. STOP.
NORIKO, I KNEW THIS MOMENT WOULD COME SOONER OR LATER.
WHAT'S GOING ON?
GO AHEAD, YOUNG MAN. DO WHAT YOU CAME TO DO. TELL HER YOU HAVEN'T FORGOTTEN WHO YOU ARE.
...
MY NAME IS ZUKO. I AM LORD OF THE FIRE NATION--
--AND I AM YOUR SON.

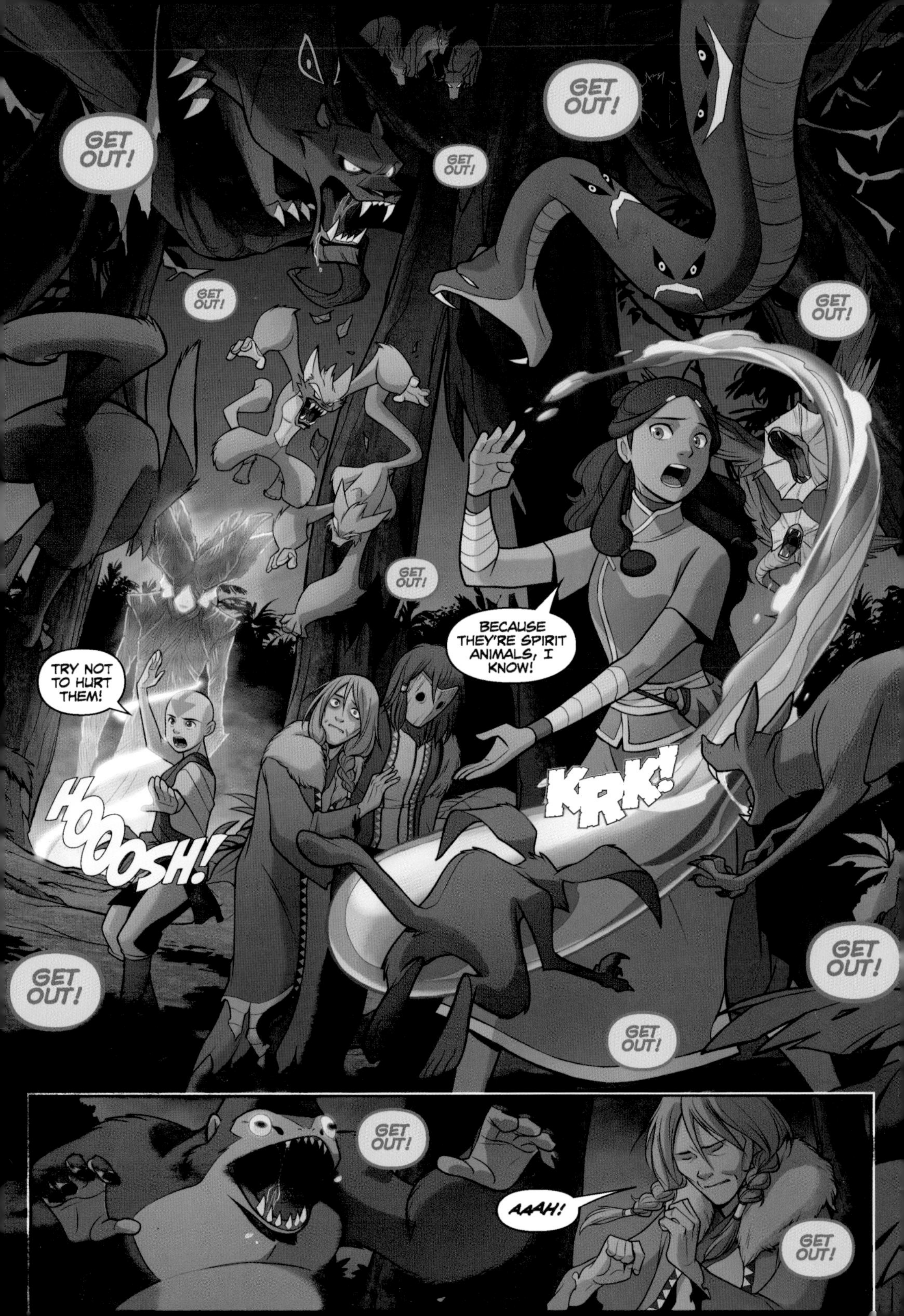

GET OUT!
GET OUT!
GET OUT!
GET OUT!
GET OUT!
GET OUT!
TRY NOT TO HURT THEM!
BECAUSE THEY'RE SPIRIT ANIMALS, I KNOW!
HOOOOSH!
KRK!
GET OUT!
GET OUT!
GET OUT!
GET OUT!
AAAH!
GET OUT!

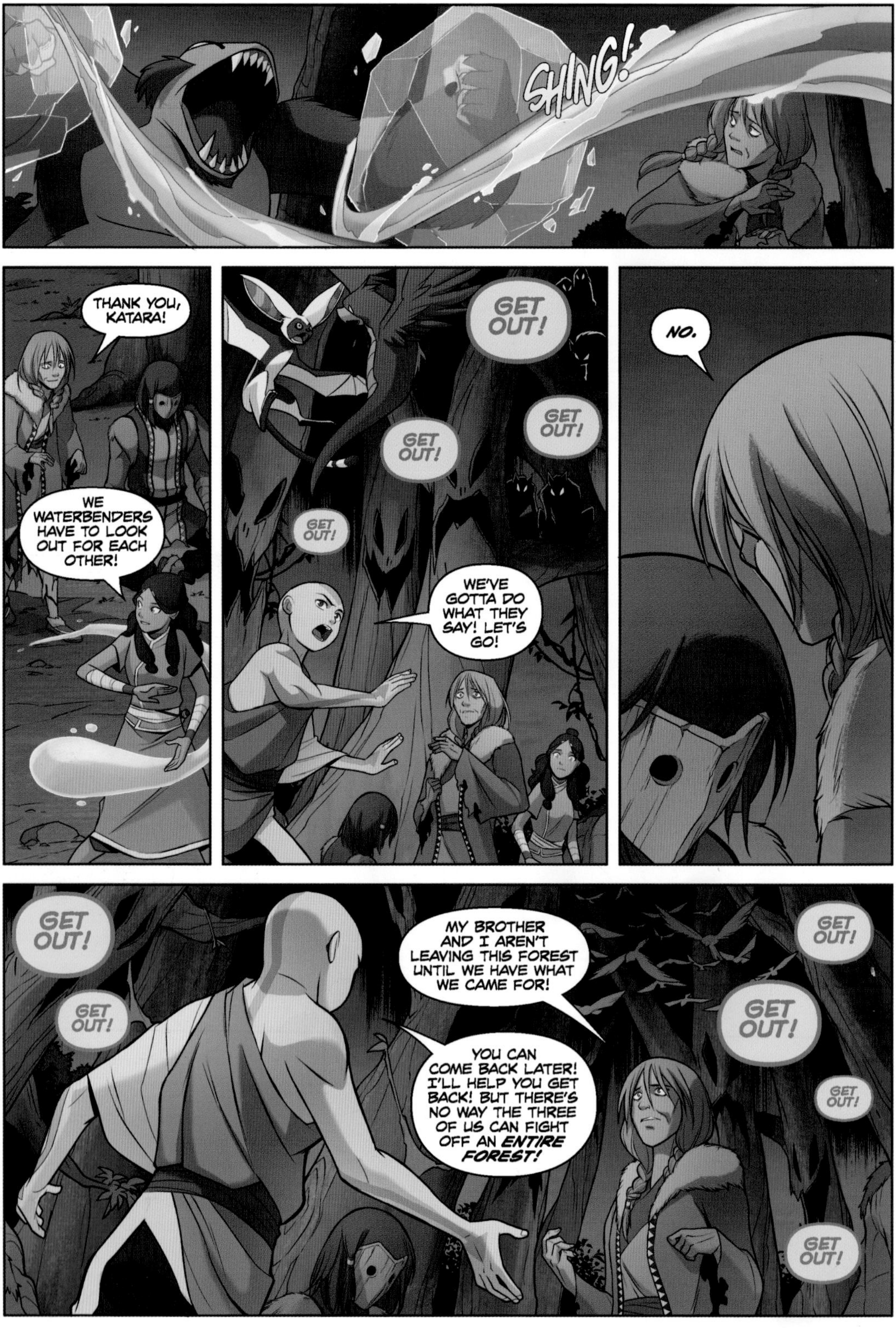
SHING!
THANK YOU, KATARA!
WE WATERBENDERS HAVE TO LOOK OUT FOR EACH OTHER!
GET OUT!
GET OUT!
GET OUT!
GET OUT!
WE'VE GOTTA DO WHAT THEY SAY! LET'S GO!
NO.
GET OUT!
GET OUT!
MY BROTHER AND I AREN'T LEAVING THIS FOREST UNTIL WE HAVE WHAT WE CAME FOR!
YOU CAN COME BACK LATER! I'LL HELP YOU GET BACK! BUT THERE'S NO WAY THE THREE OF US CAN FIGHT OFF AN ENTIRE FOREST!
GET OUT!
GET OUT!
GET OUT!
GET OUT!

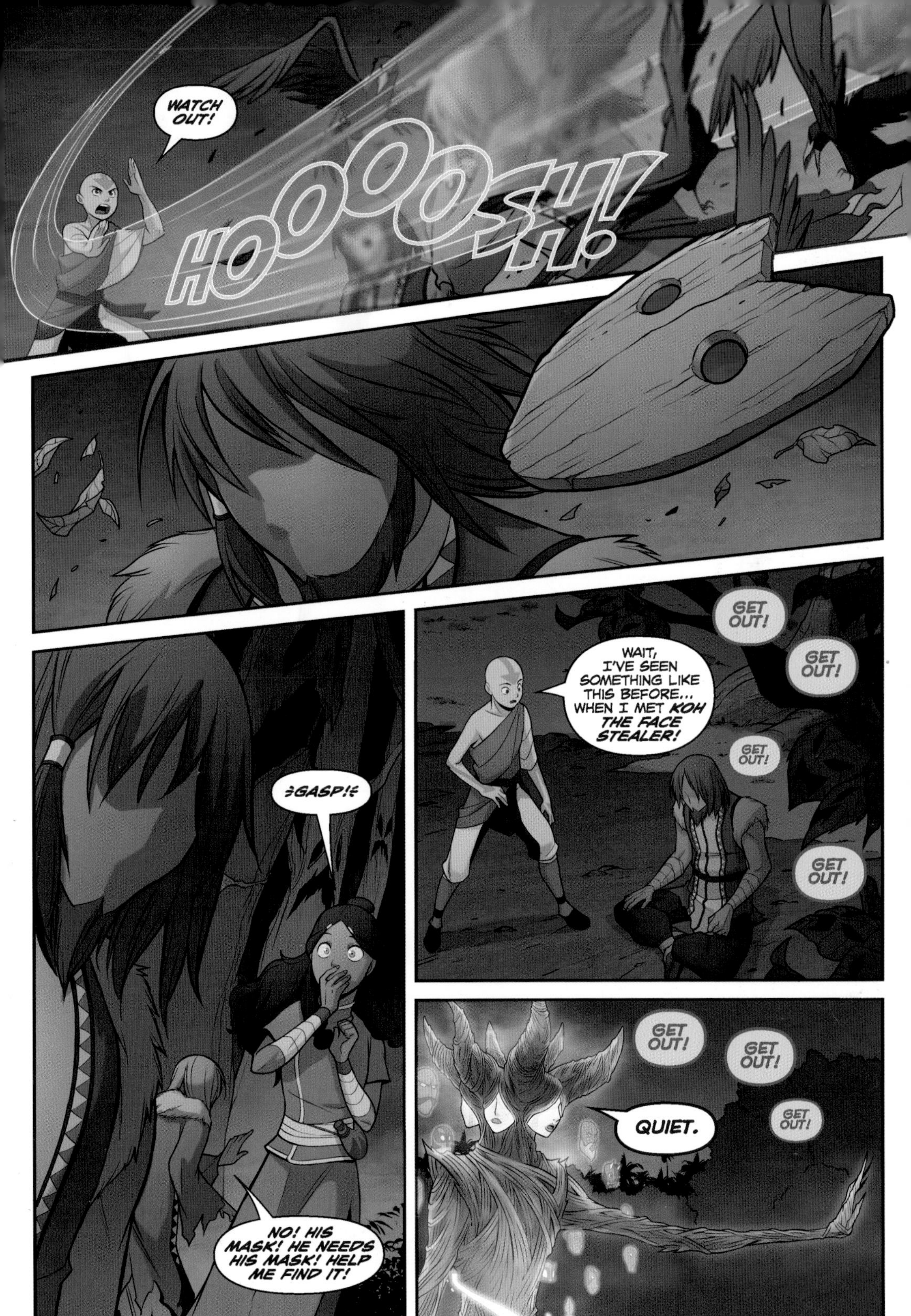
WATCH OUT!
HOOOOOSH!
GET OUT!
GET OUT!
WAIT, I'VE SEEN SOMETHING LIKE THIS BEFORE... WHEN I MET KOH THE FACE STEALER!
GET OUT!
GET OUT!
GASP!
NO! HIS MASK! HE NEEDS HIS MASK! HELP ME FIND IT!
GET OUT!
GET OUT!
GET OUT!
QUIET.

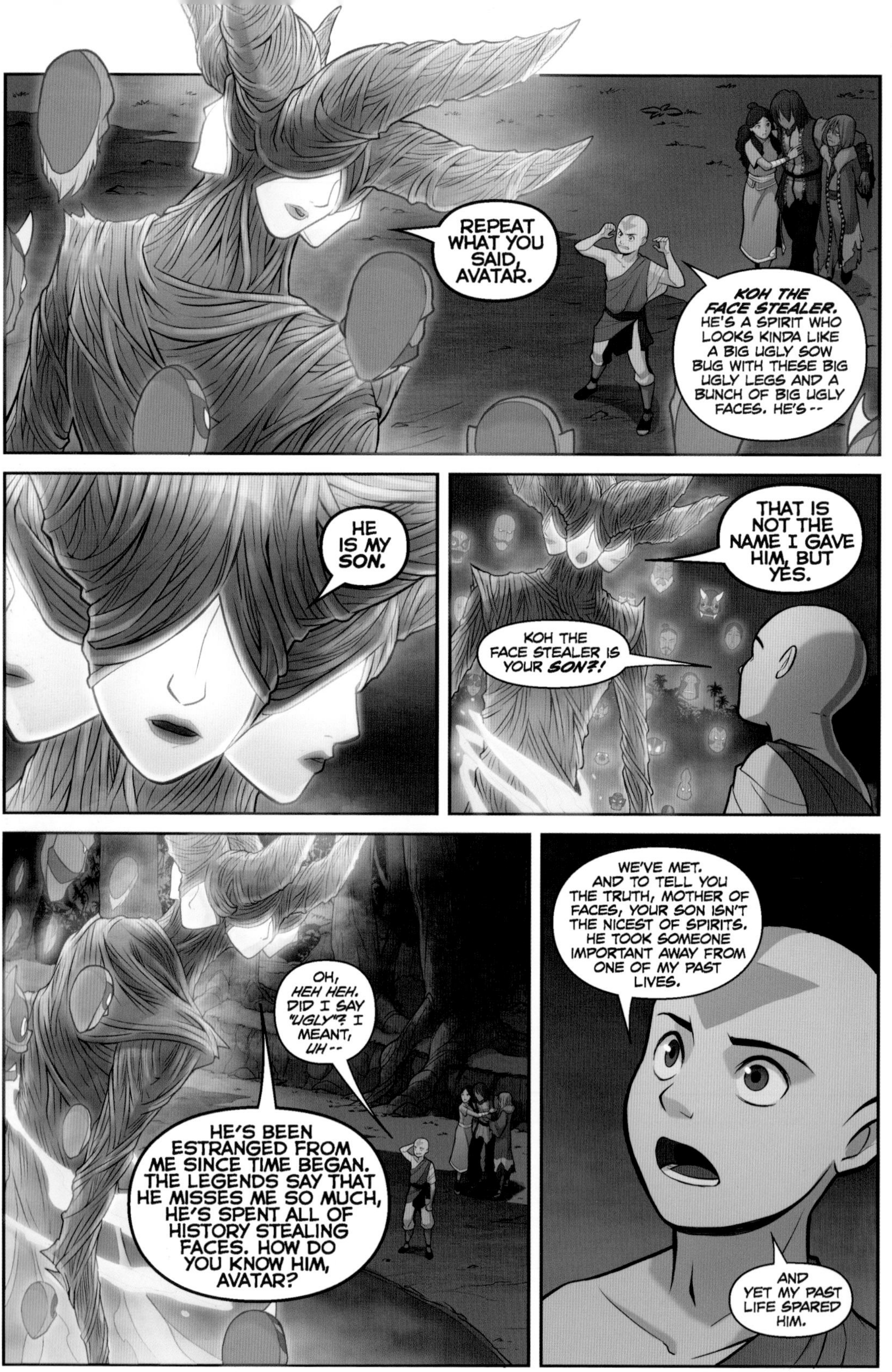
REPEAT WHAT YOU SAID, AVATAR.
KOH THE FACE STEALER. HE'S A SPIRIT WHO LOOKS KINDA LIKE A BIG UGLY SOW BUG WITH THESE BIG UGLY LEGS AND A BUNCH OF BIG UGLY FACES. HE'S --
HE IS MY SON.
THAT IS NOT THE NAME I GAVE HIM, BUT YES.
KOH THE FACE STEALER IS YOUR SON?!
OH, HEH HEH. DID I SAY "UGLY"? I MEANT, UH --
HE'S BEEN ESTRANGED FROM ME SINCE TIME BEGAN. THE LEGENDS SAY THAT HE MISSES ME SO MUCH, HE'S SPENT ALL OF HISTORY STEALING FACES. HOW DO YOU KNOW HIM, AVATAR?
WE'VE MET. AND TO TELL YOU THE TRUTH, MOTHER OF FACES, YOUR SON ISN'T THE NICEST OF SPIRITS. HE TOOK SOMEONE IMPORTANT AWAY FROM ONE OF MY PAST LIVES.
AND YET MY PAST LIFE SPARED HIM.

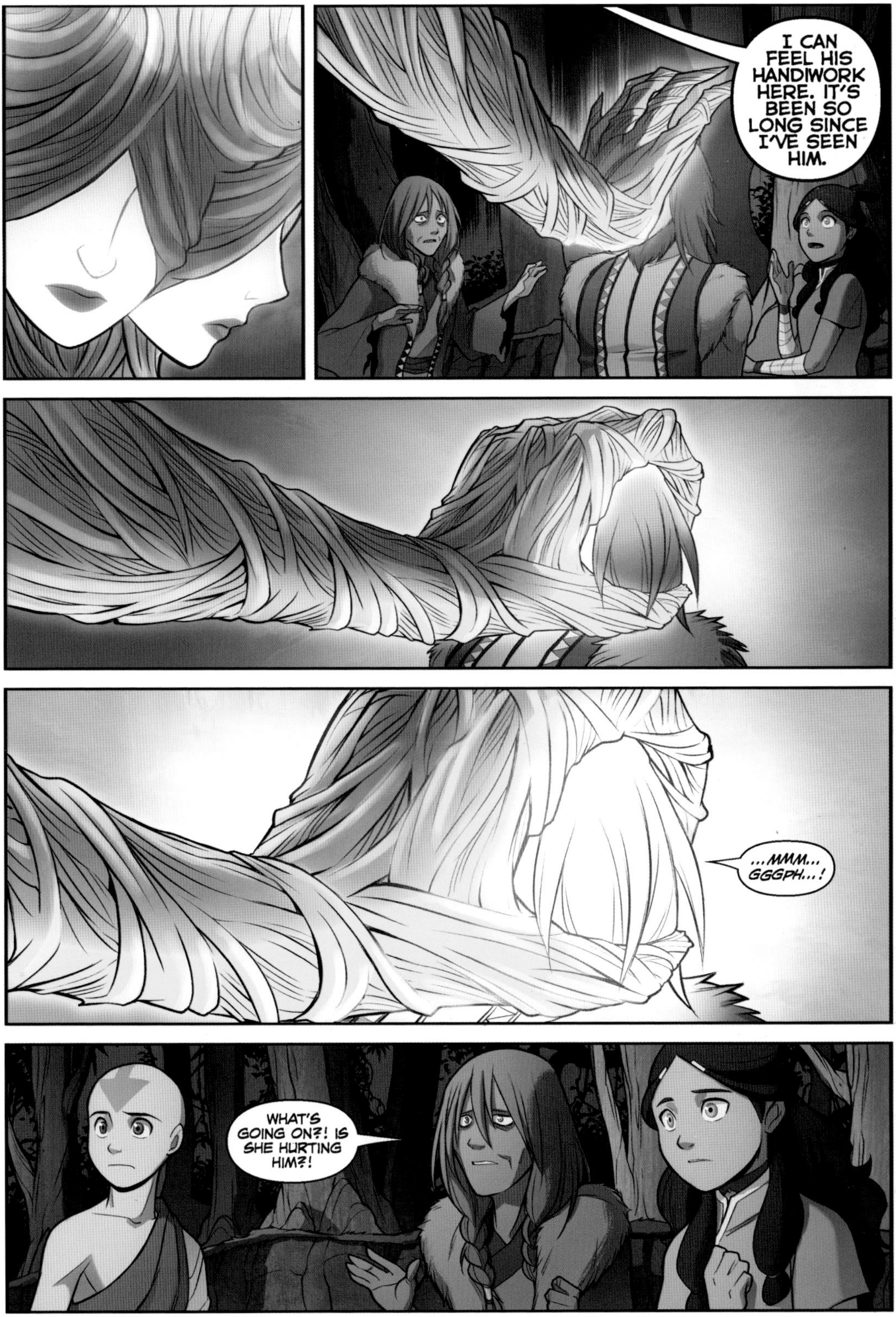
I CAN FEEL HIS HANDIWORK HERE. IT'S BEEN SO LONG SINCE I'VE SEEN HIM.
...MMM... GGGPH...!
WHAT'S GOING ON?! IS SHE HURTING HIM?!

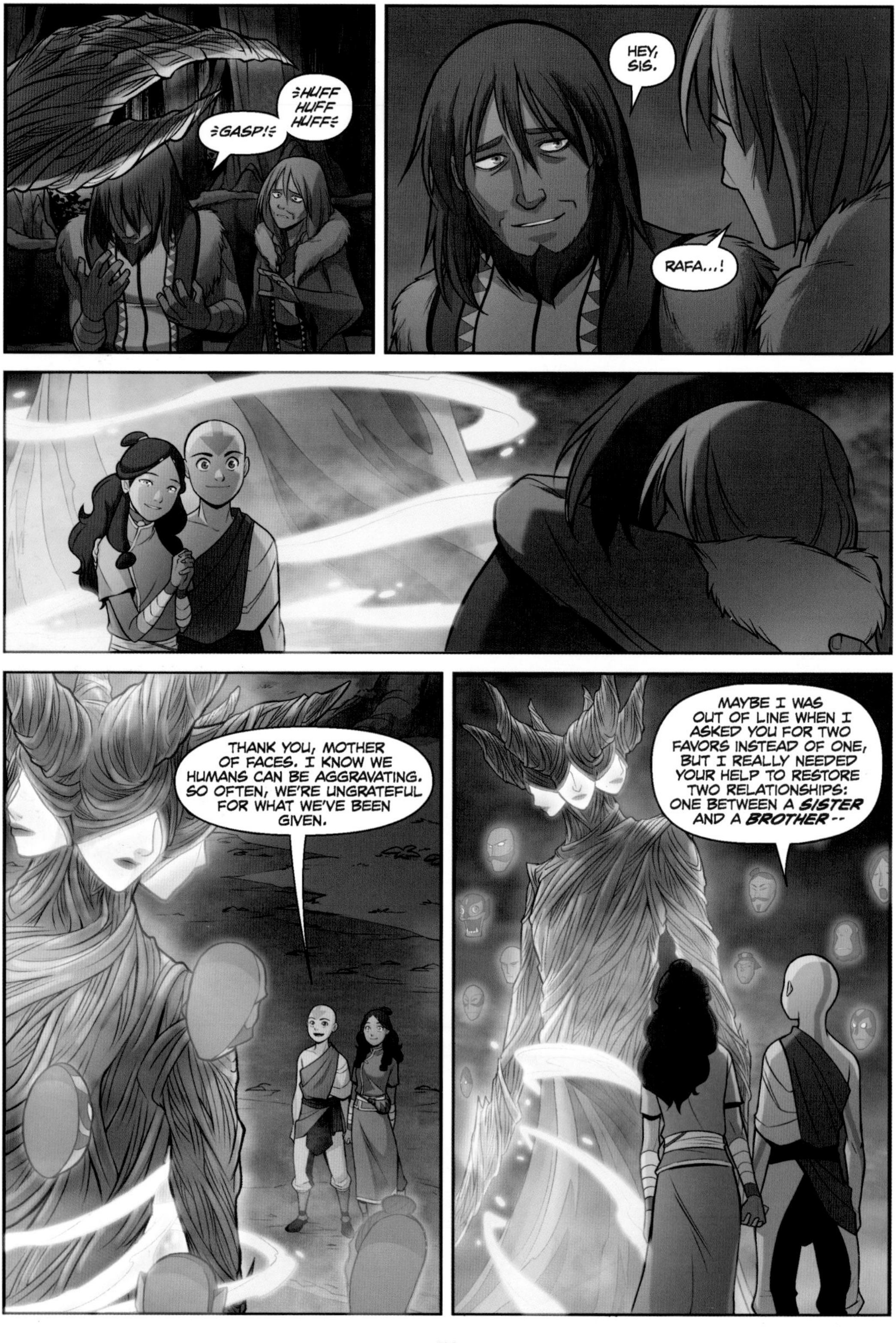

HUFF HUFF HUFF
GASP!
HEY, SIS.
RAFA...!
THANK YOU, MOTHER OF FACES. I KNOW WE HUMANS CAN BE AGGRAVATING. SO OFTEN, WE'RE UNGRATEFUL FOR WHAT WE'VE BEEN GIVEN.
MAYBE I WAS OUT OF LINE WHEN I ASKED YOU FOR TWO FAVORS INSTEAD OF ONE, BUT I REALLY NEEDED YOUR HELP TO RESTORE TWO RELATIONSHIPS: ONE BETWEEN A ***SISTER*** AND A ***BROTHER*** --

-- AND ANOTHER BETWEEN A *MOTHER* AND A *SON*.

WHEN I SAW YOU IN THE CROWD, I RECOGNIZED YOU IMMEDIATELY BECAUSE OF YOUR SCAR. I HAD LEARNED ALL I COULD ABOUT URSA'S LIFE IN THE ROYAL PALACE. I KNEW IT WOULD COME BACK TO HAUNT US SOMEDAY.

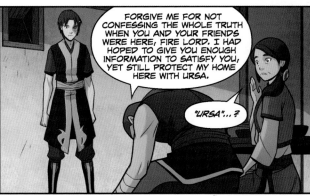

FORGIVE ME FOR NOT CONFESSING THE WHOLE TRUTH WHEN YOU AND YOUR FRIENDS WERE HERE, FIRE LORD. I HAD HOPED TO GIVE YOU ENOUGH INFORMATION TO SATISFY YOU, YET STILL PROTECT MY HOME HERE WITH URSA.

*"URSA"...?*

THAT WAS YOUR OLD NAME, MY LOVE, FROM YOUR OLD LIFE.

YOU WERE ONCE A PRINCESS OF THE FIRE NATION. YOU HAD TWO CHILDREN, ONE OF WHOM GREW UP TO BE THE FIRE LORD.

MOMMY? WHAT'S DADDY TALKING ABOUT?

YOU DON'T REMEMBER ANY OF THIS BECAUSE A POWERFUL SPIRIT ALTERED YOUR MEMORIES.

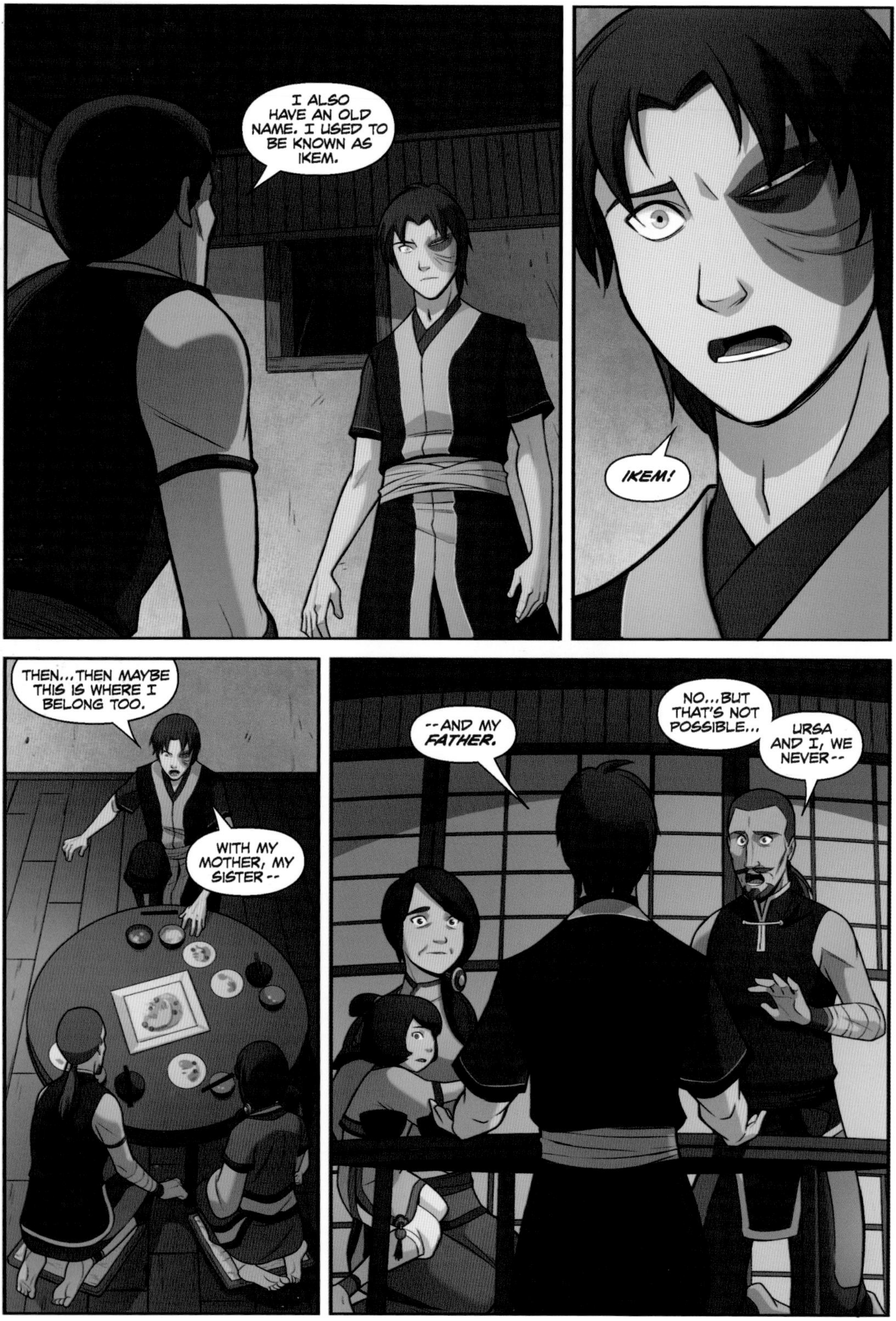
I ALSO HAVE AN OLD NAME. I USED TO BE KNOWN AS IKEM.
IKEM!
THEN...THEN MAYBE THIS IS WHERE I BELONG TOO.
WITH MY MOTHER, MY SISTER --
--AND MY FATHER.
NO...BUT THAT'S NOT POSSIBLE...
URSA AND I, WE NEVER--

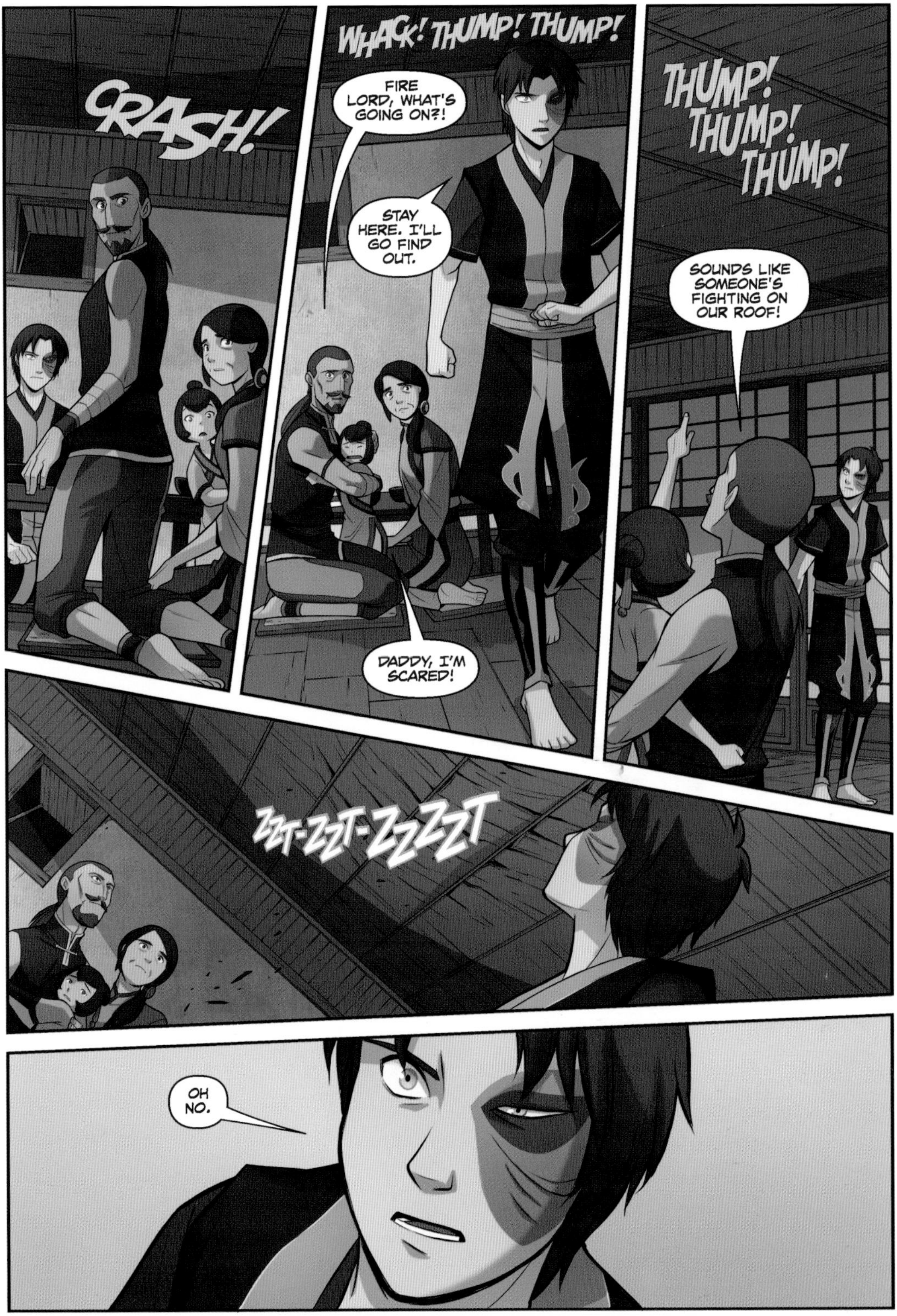
CRASH!
WHACK! THUMP! THUMP!
FIRE LORD, WHAT'S GOING ON?!
STAY HERE. I'LL GO FIND OUT.
DADDY, I'M SCARED!
THUMP! THUMP! THUMP!
SOUNDS LIKE SOMEONE'S FIGHTING ON OUR ROOF!
ZZZT-ZZZT-ZZZZZT
OH NO.

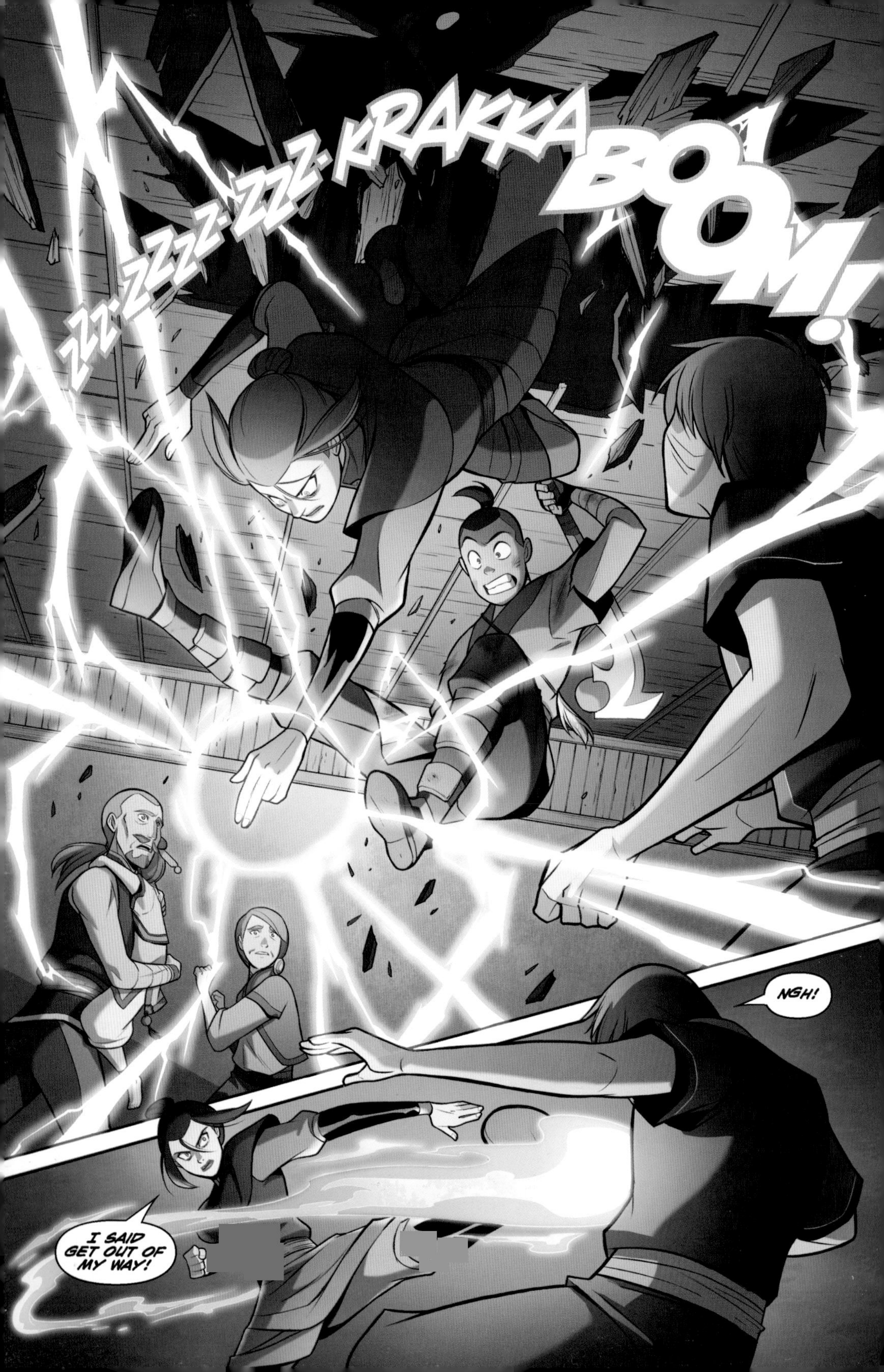
ZZZ-ZZZZZ-ZZZ-KRAKKA
BOOM!
NGH!
I SAID GET OUT OF MY WAY!

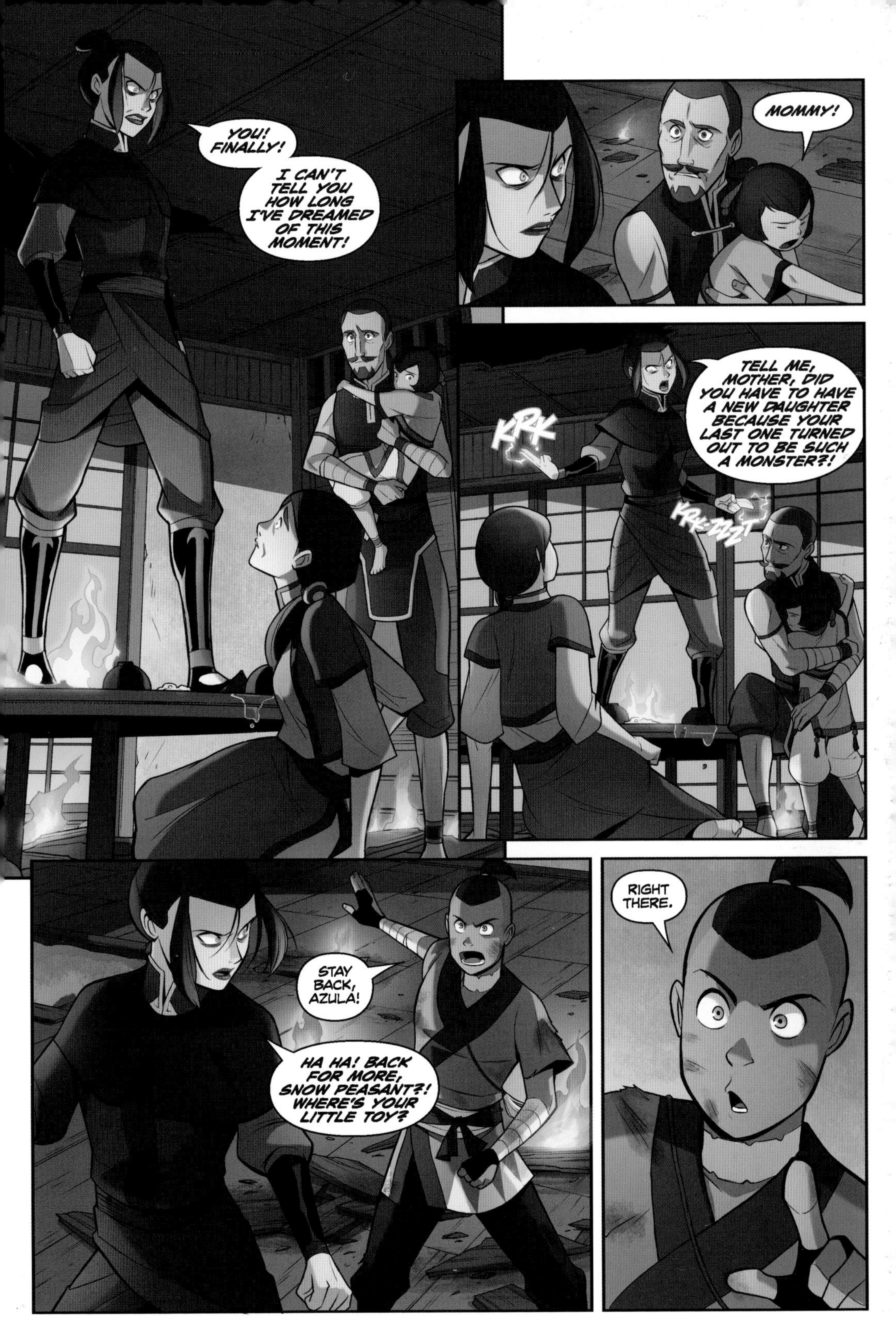
YOU! FINALLY!
I CAN'T TELL YOU HOW LONG I'VE DREAMED OF THIS MOMENT!
MOMMY!
TELL ME, MOTHER, DID YOU HAVE TO HAVE A NEW DAUGHTER BECAUSE YOUR LAST ONE TURNED OUT TO BE SUCH A MONSTER?!
KRK
KRK-ZZZT
STAY BACK, AZULA!
HA HA! BACK FOR MORE, SNOW PEASANT?! WHERE'S YOUR LITTLE TOY?
RIGHT THERE.

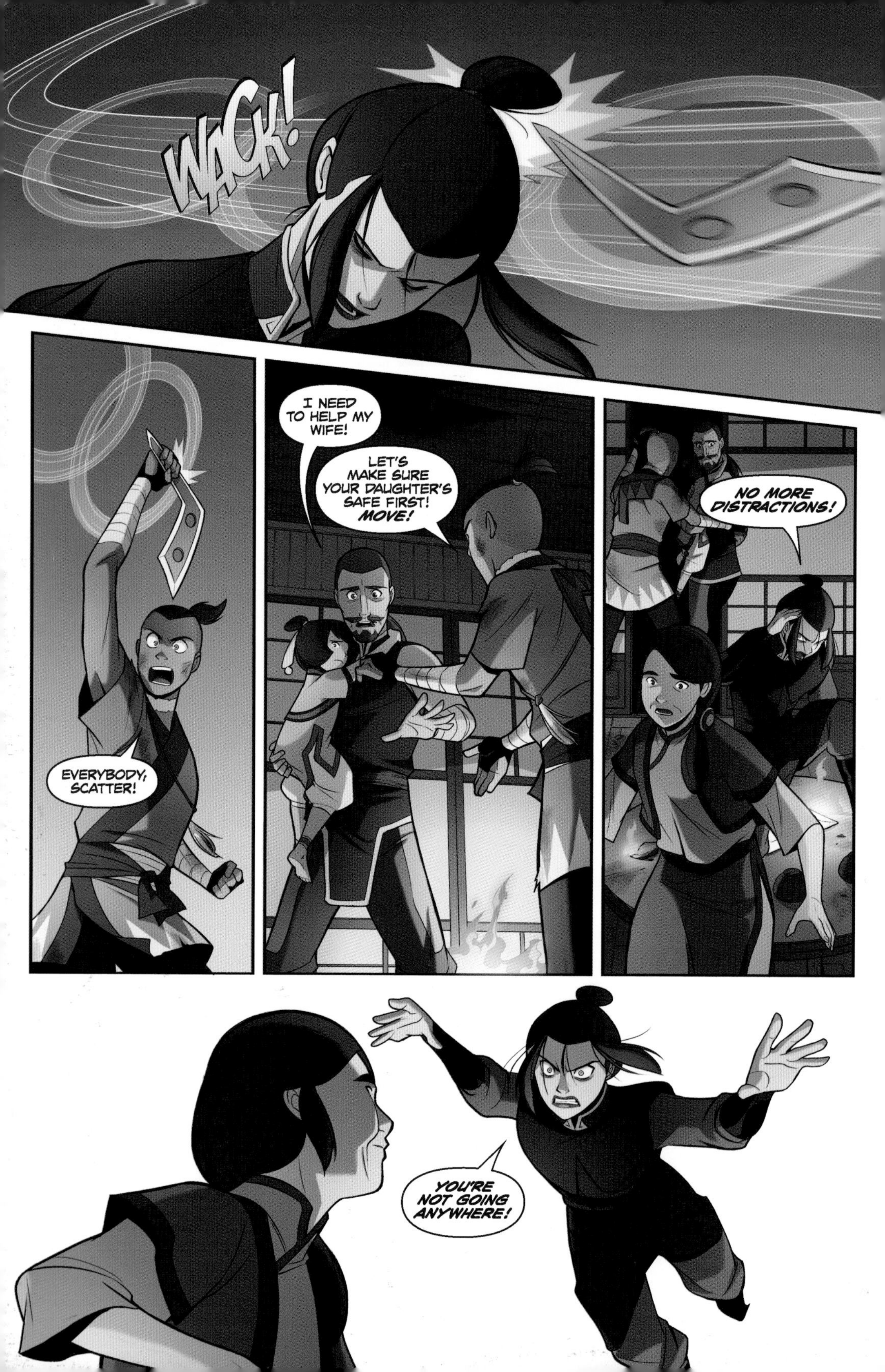
WACK!
EVERYBODY, SCATTER!
I NEED TO HELP MY WIFE!
LET'S MAKE SURE YOUR DAUGHTER'S SAFE FIRST! MOVE!
NO MORE DISTRACTIONS!
YOU'RE NOT GOING ANYWHERE!

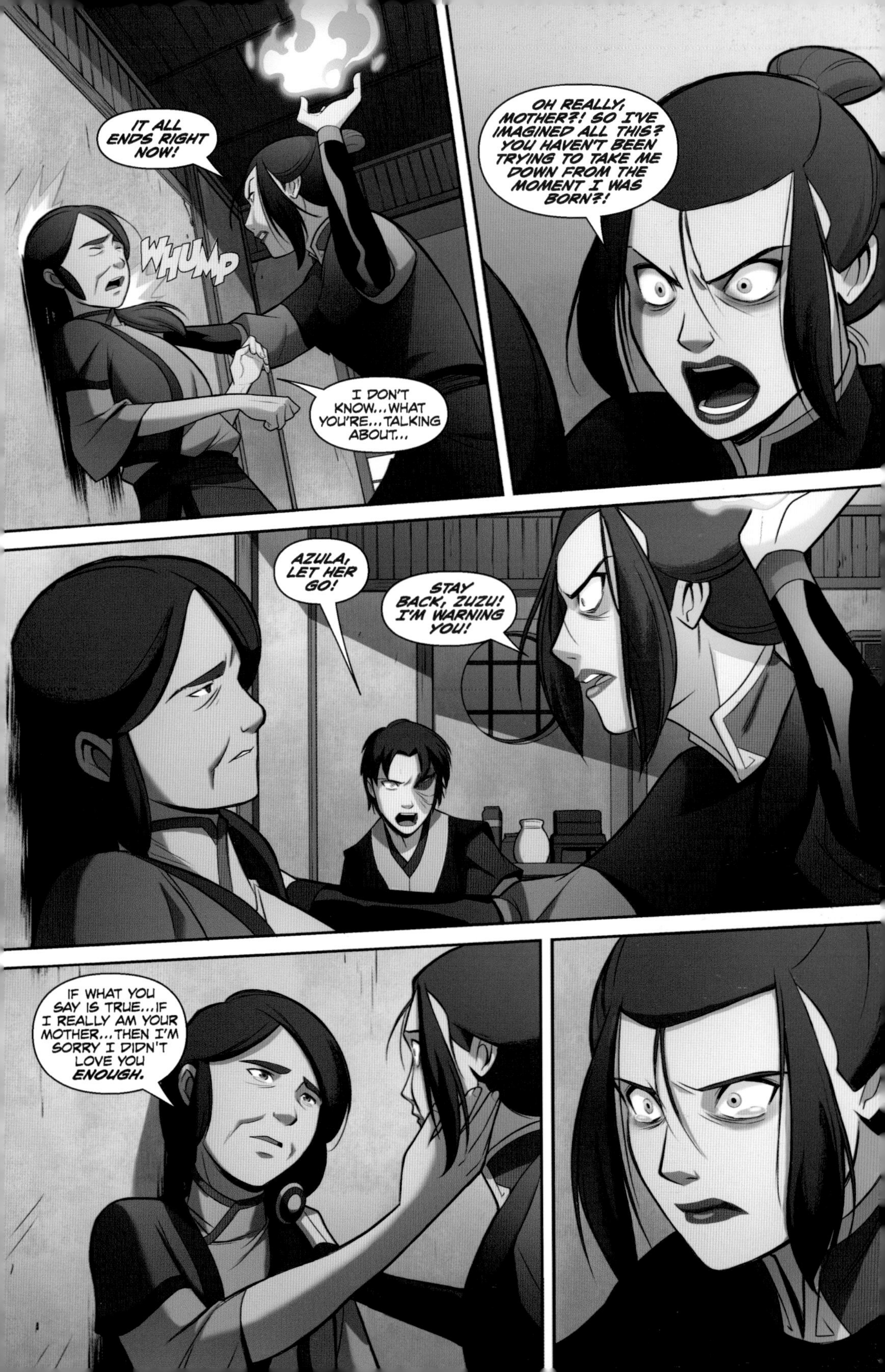
IT ALL ENDS RIGHT NOW!
WHUMP
I DON'T KNOW...WHAT YOU'RE...TALKING ABOUT...
OH REALLY, MOTHER?! SO I'VE IMAGINED ALL THIS? YOU HAVEN'T BEEN TRYING TO TAKE ME DOWN FROM THE MOMENT I WAS BORN?!
AZULA, LET HER GO!
STAY BACK, ZUZU! I'M WARNING YOU!
IF WHAT YOU SAY IS TRUE...IF I REALLY AM YOUR MOTHER...THEN I'M SORRY I DIDN'T LOVE YOU ENOUGH.

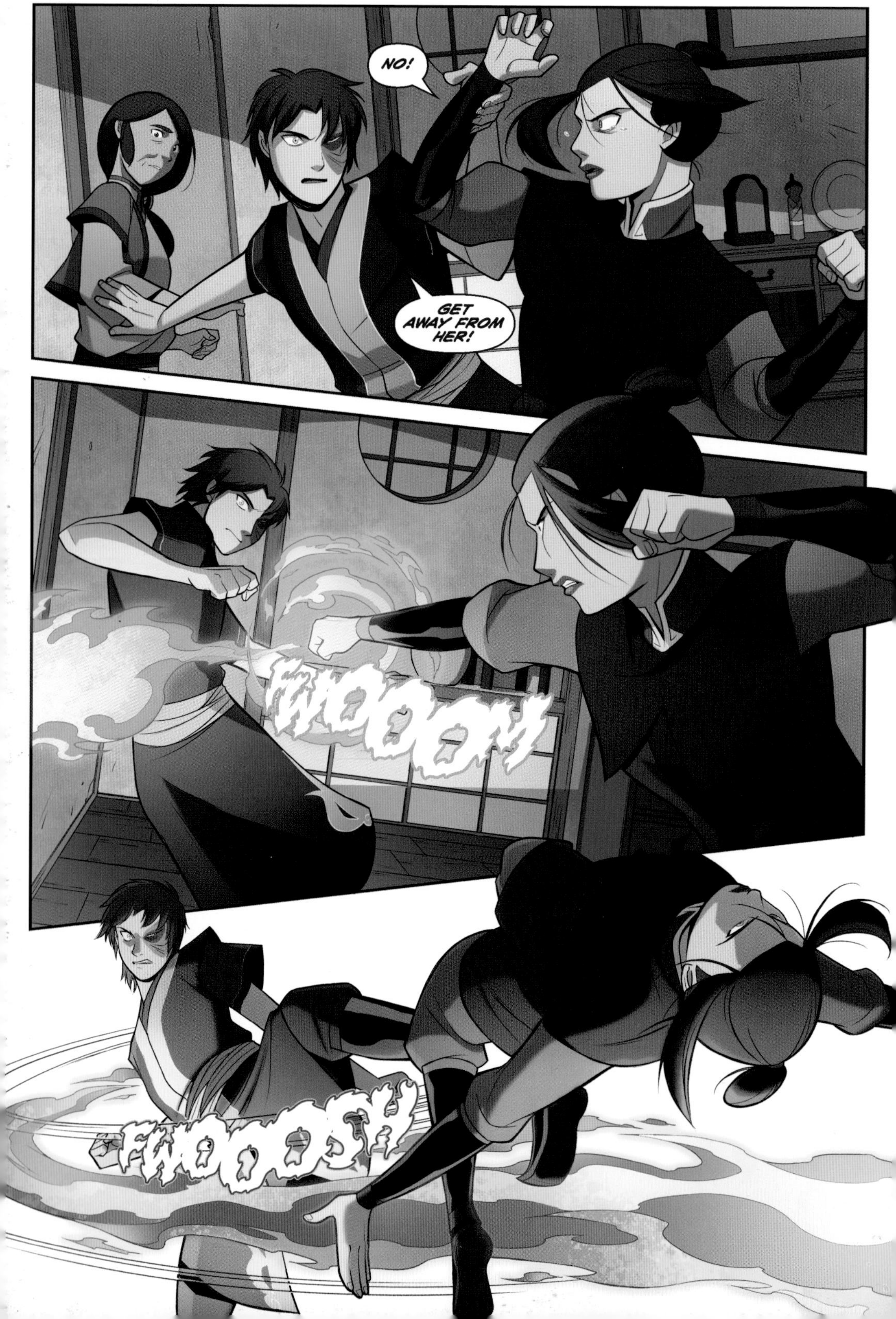
NO!
GET AWAY FROM HER!
FWOOOM
FWOOOSH

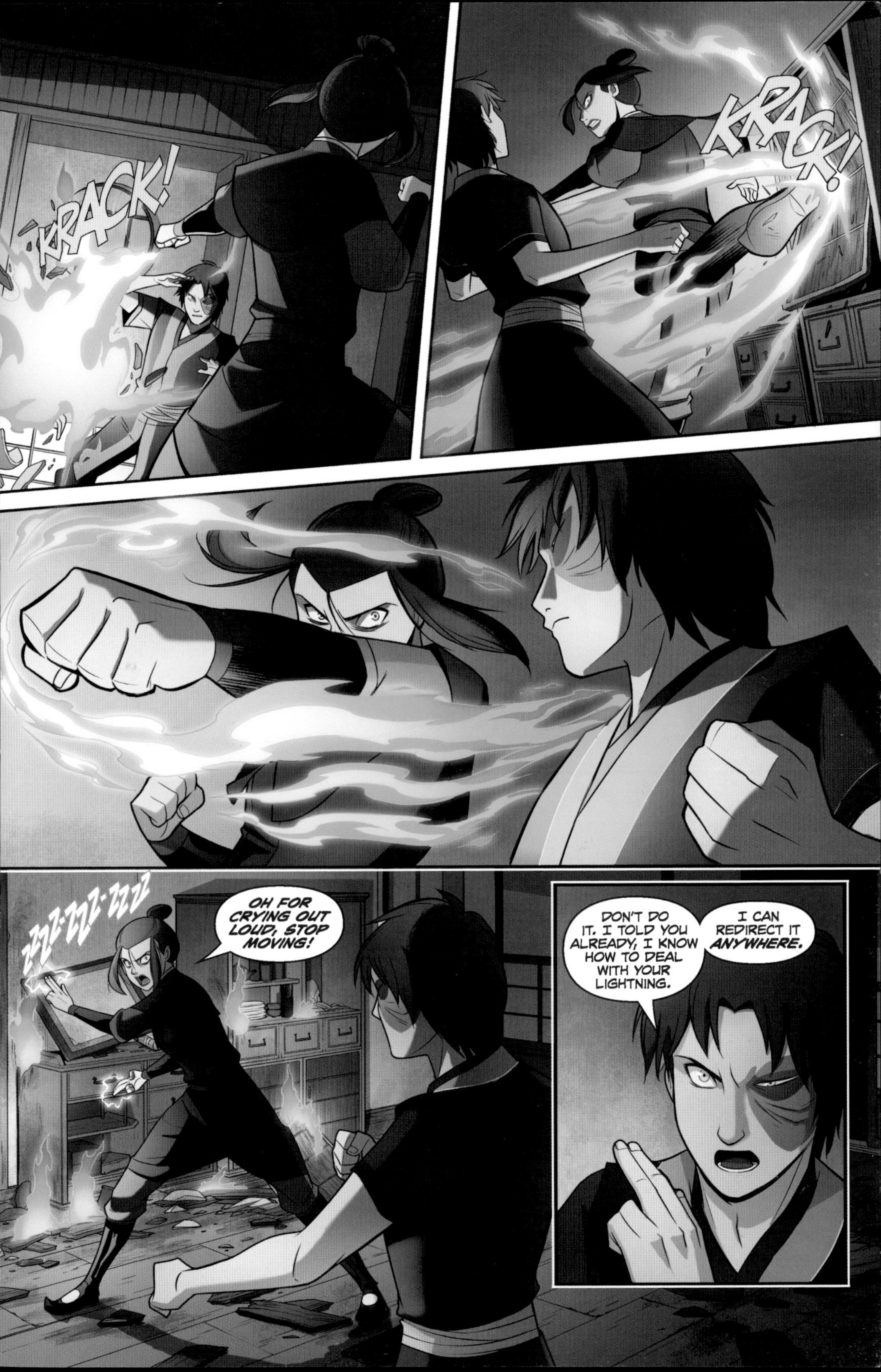
KRACK!
KRACK!
ZZZZ-ZZZ-ZZZZ
OH FOR CRYING OUT LOUD, STOP MOVING!
DON'T DO IT. I TOLD YOU ALREADY, I KNOW HOW TO DEAL WITH YOUR LIGHTNING.
I CAN REDIRECT IT *ANYWHERE.*

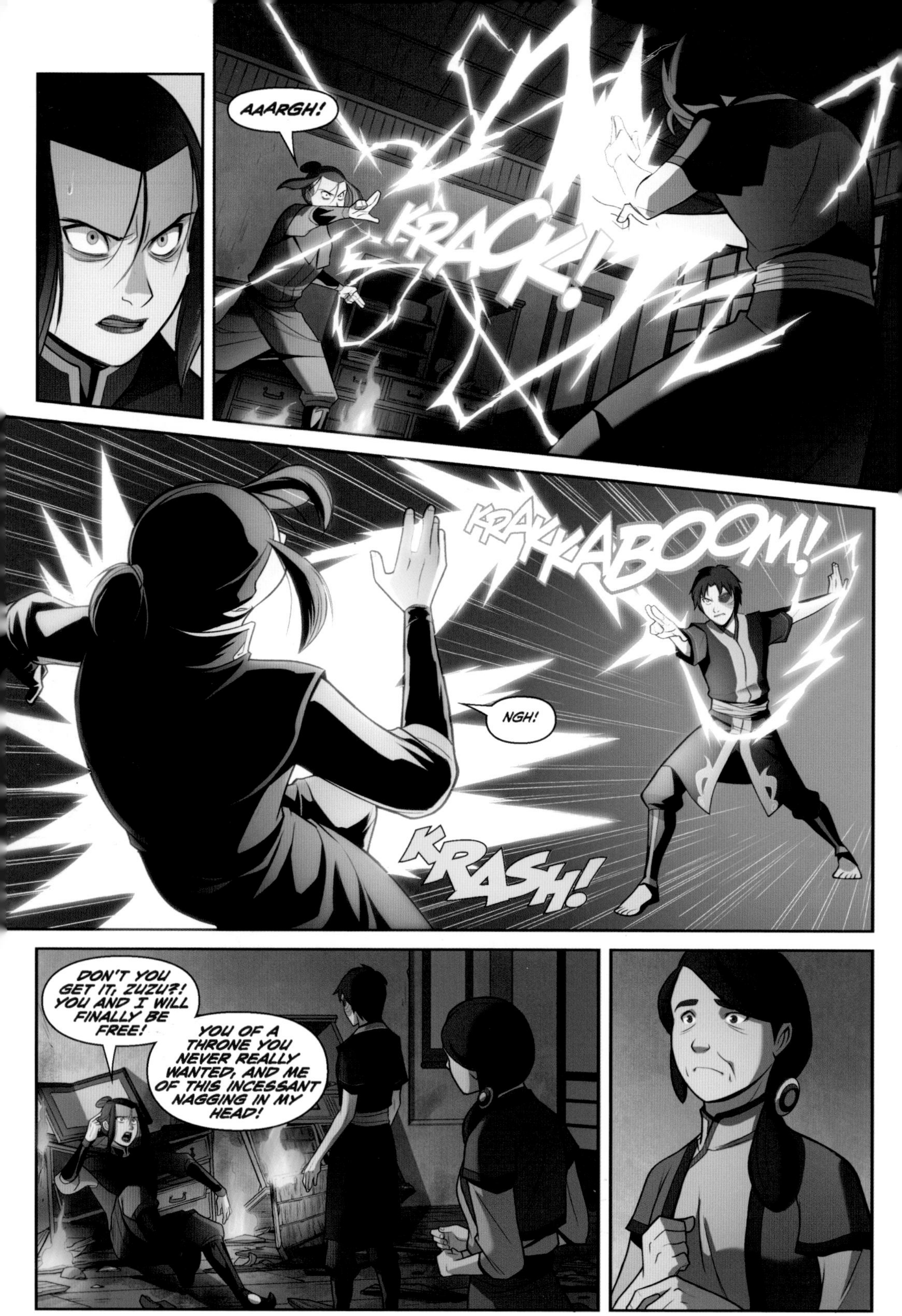
AAARGH!
KRACK!
KRAKKABOOM!
NGH!
KRASH!
DON'T YOU GET IT, ZUZU?! YOU AND I WILL FINALLY BE FREE!
YOU OF A THRONE YOU NEVER REALLY WANTED, AND ME OF THIS INCESSANT NAGGING IN MY HEAD!

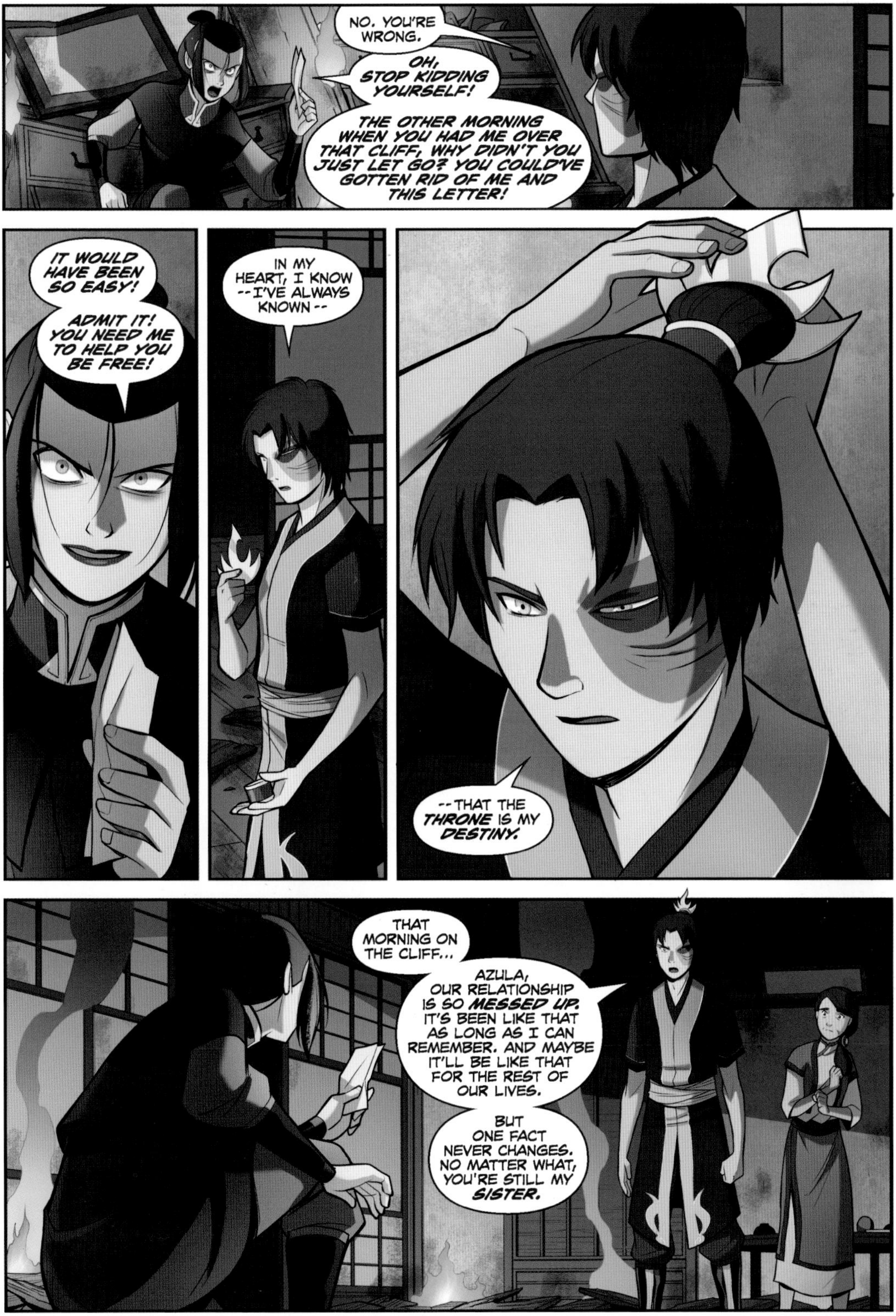
NO. YOU'RE WRONG.
OH, STOP KIDDING YOURSELF!
THE OTHER MORNING WHEN YOU HAD ME OVER THAT CLIFF, WHY DIDN'T YOU JUST LET GO? YOU COULD'VE GOTTEN RID OF ME AND THIS LETTER!
IT WOULD HAVE BEEN SO EASY!
ADMIT IT! YOU NEED ME TO HELP YOU BE FREE!
IN MY HEART, I KNOW --I'VE ALWAYS KNOWN--
--THAT THE THRONE IS MY DESTINY.
THAT MORNING ON THE CLIFF...
AZULA, OUR RELATIONSHIP IS SO MESSED UP. IT'S BEEN LIKE THAT AS LONG AS I CAN REMEMBER. AND MAYBE IT'LL BE LIKE THAT FOR THE REST OF OUR LIVES.
BUT ONE FACT NEVER CHANGES. NO MATTER WHAT, YOU'RE STILL MY SISTER.

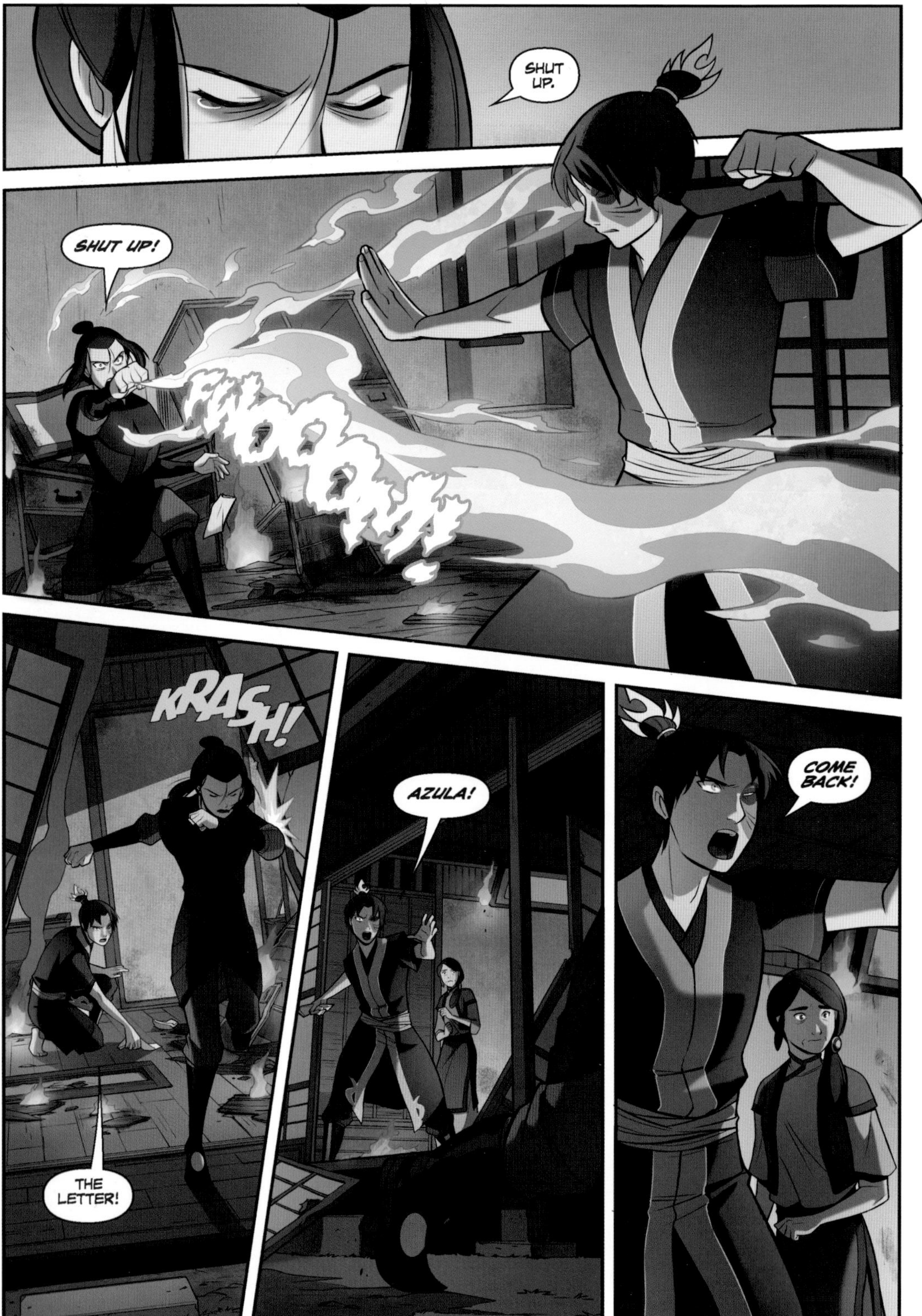
SHUT UP.
SHUT UP!
FWOOOM!
KRASH!
THE LETTER!
AZULA!
COME BACK!

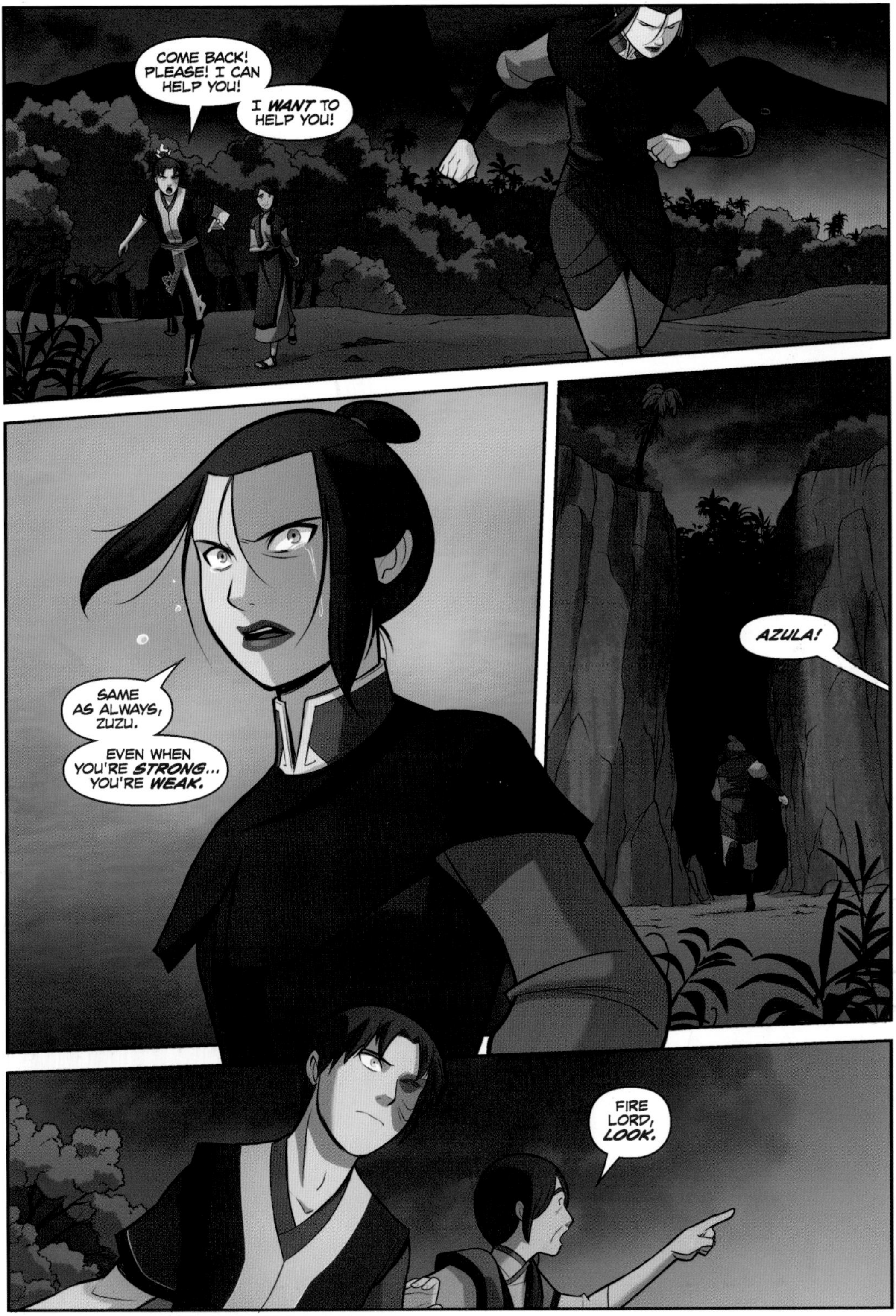
COME BACK! PLEASE! I CAN HELP YOU!
I *WANT* TO HELP YOU!
SAME AS ALWAYS, ZUZU.
EVEN WHEN YOU'RE *STRONG*... YOU'RE *WEAK*.
*AZULA!*
FIRE LORD, *LOOK*.

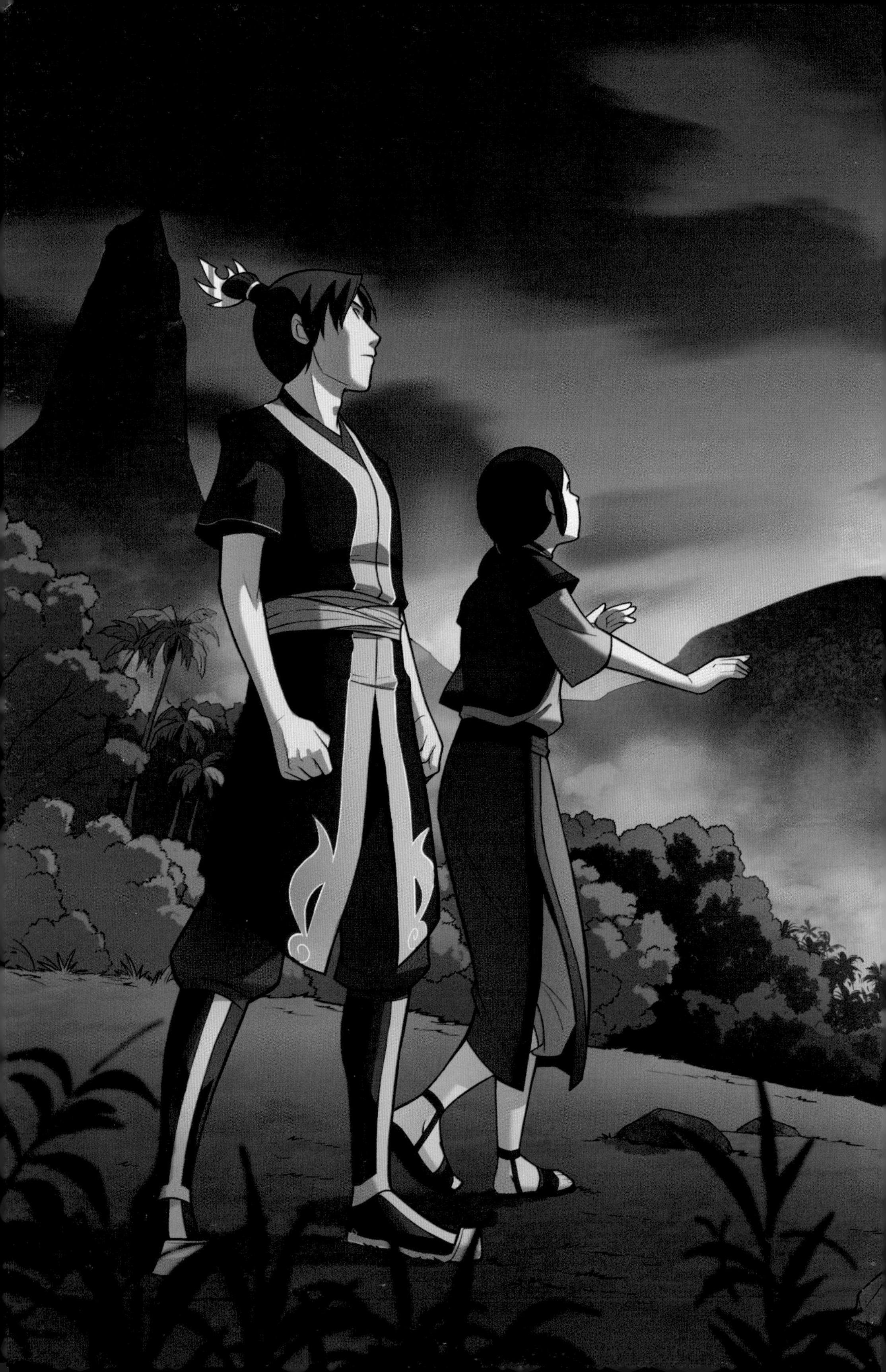

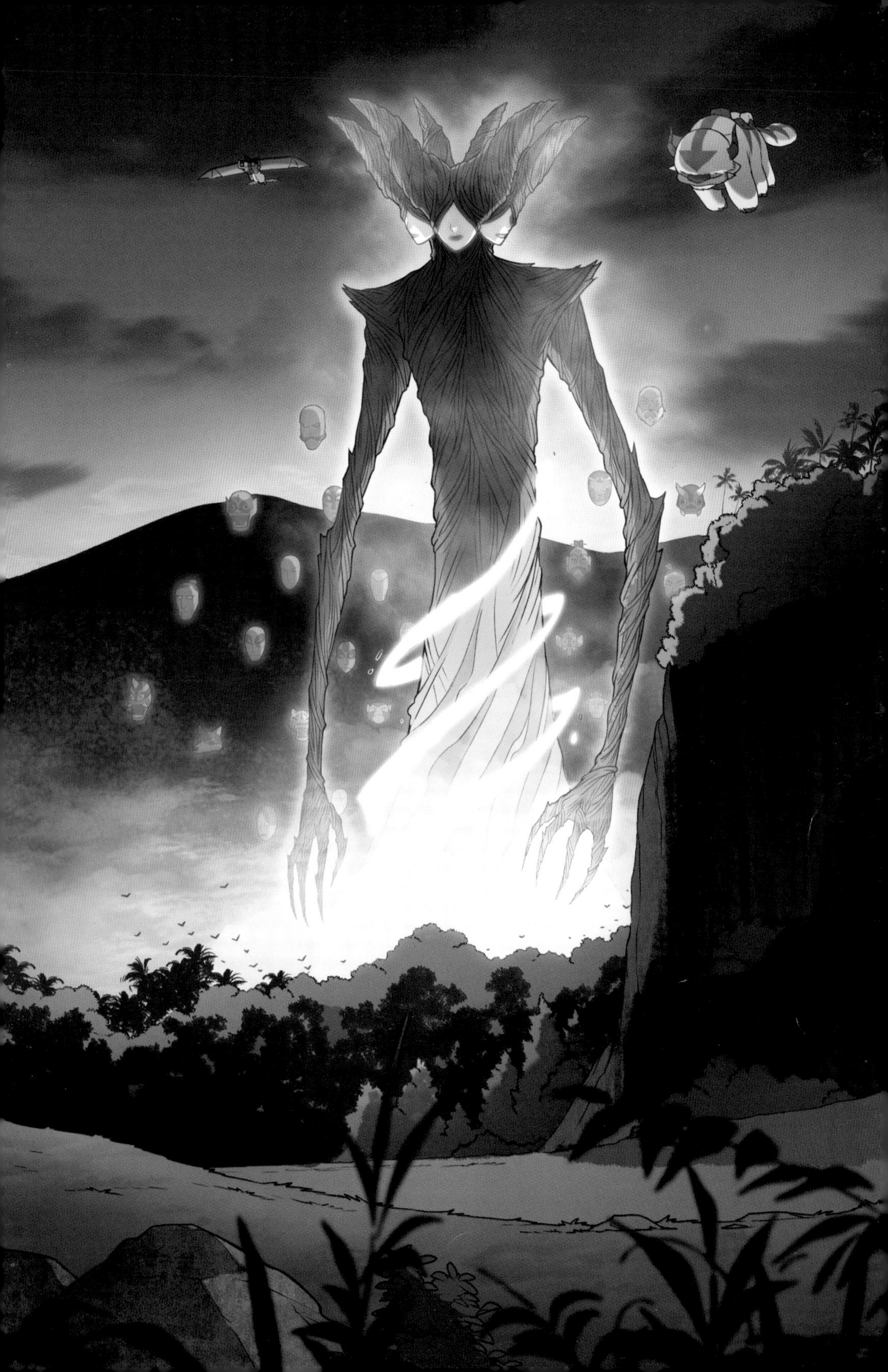

HUMAN, DO YOU WISH TO RETURN TO WHO YOU ONCE WERE?

DO YOU WISH TO *REMEMBER?*

NO, YOU DON'T HAVE TO. YOU HAVE SUCH A BEAUTIFUL LIFE HERE.

YES.

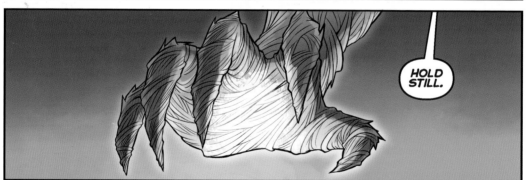

HOLD STILL.

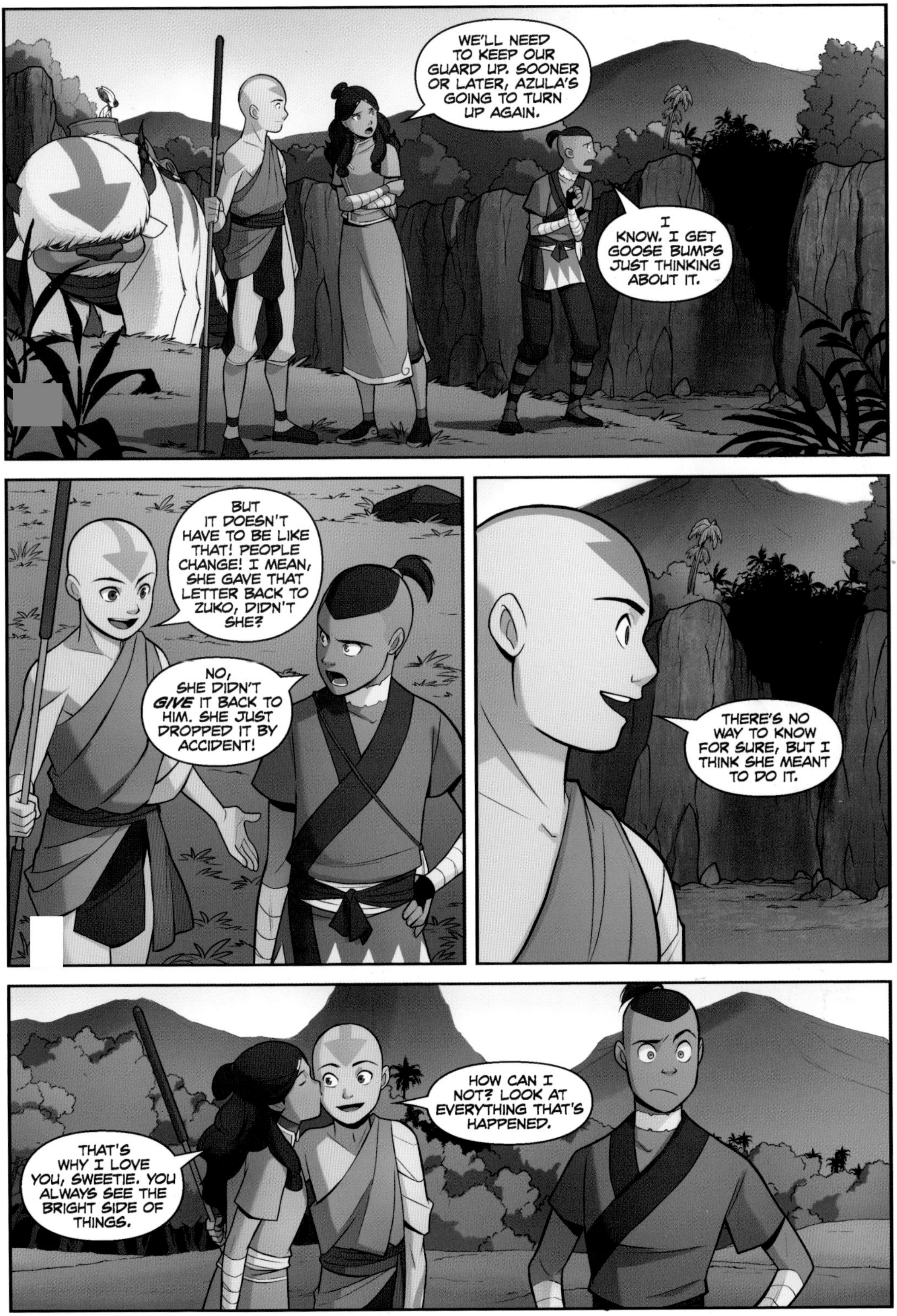
WE'LL NEED TO KEEP OUR GUARD UP. SOONER OR LATER, AZULA'S GOING TO TURN UP AGAIN.
I KNOW. I GET GOOSE BUMPS JUST THINKING ABOUT IT.
BUT IT DOESN'T HAVE TO BE LIKE THAT! PEOPLE CHANGE! I MEAN, SHE GAVE THAT LETTER BACK TO ZUKO, DIDN'T SHE?
NO, SHE DIDN'T *GIVE* IT BACK TO HIM. SHE JUST DROPPED IT BY ACCIDENT!
THERE'S NO WAY TO KNOW FOR SURE, BUT I THINK SHE MEANT TO DO IT.
HOW CAN I NOT? LOOK AT EVERYTHING THAT'S HAPPENED.
THAT'S WHY I LOVE YOU, SWEETIE. YOU ALWAYS SEE THE BRIGHT SIDE OF THINGS.

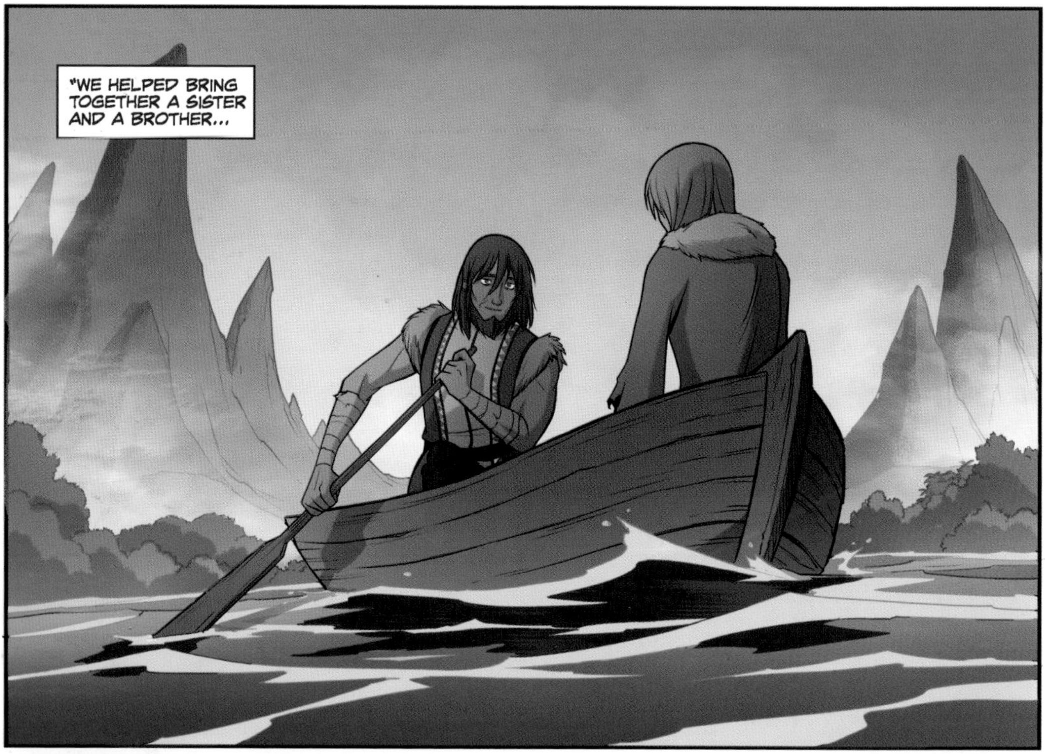
"WE HELPED BRING TOGETHER A SISTER AND A BROTHER...

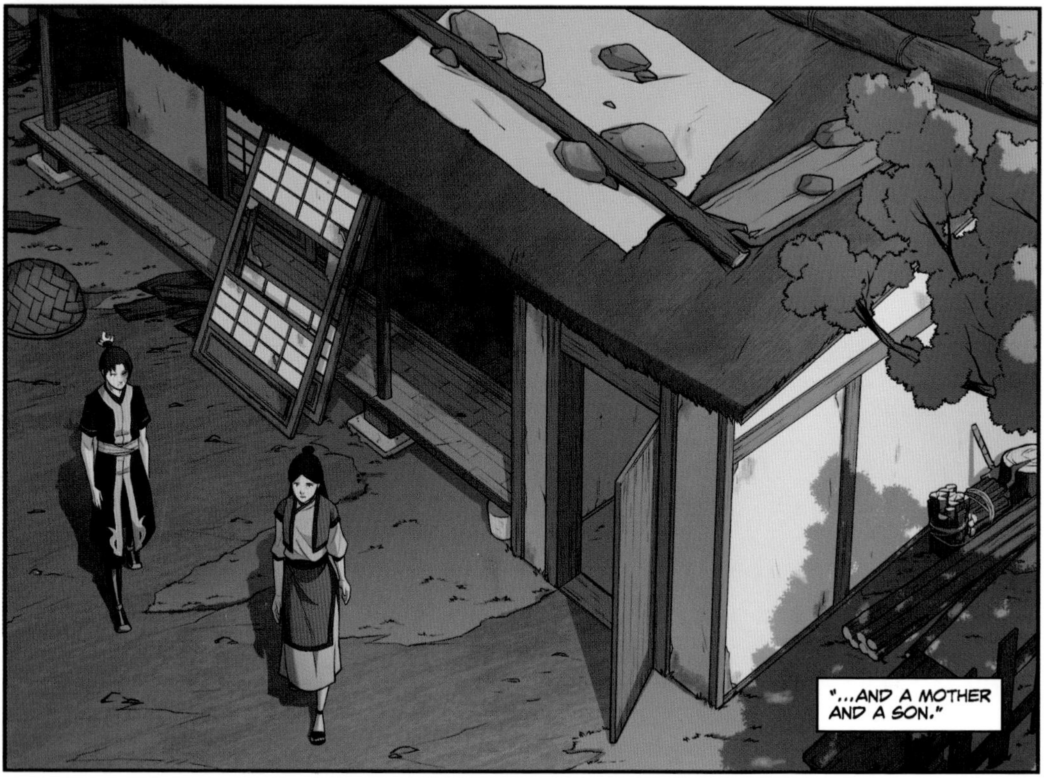
"...AND A MOTHER AND A SON."

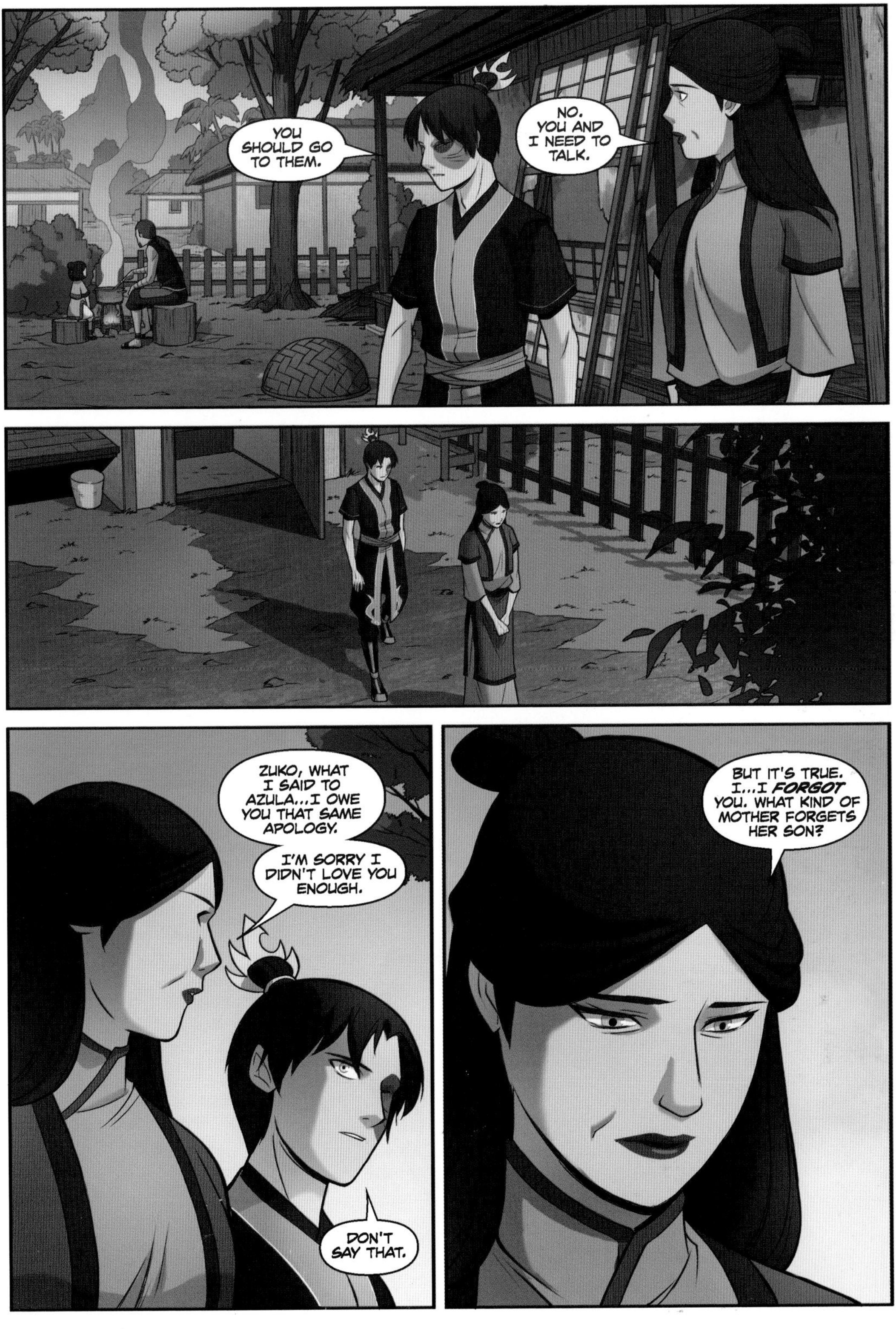
YOU SHOULD GO TO THEM.
NO. YOU AND I NEED TO TALK.
ZUKO, WHAT I SAID TO AZULA...I OWE YOU THAT SAME APOLOGY.
I'M SORRY I DIDN'T LOVE YOU ENOUGH.
DON'T SAY THAT.
BUT IT'S TRUE. I...I *FORGOT* YOU. WHAT KIND OF MOTHER FORGETS HER SON?

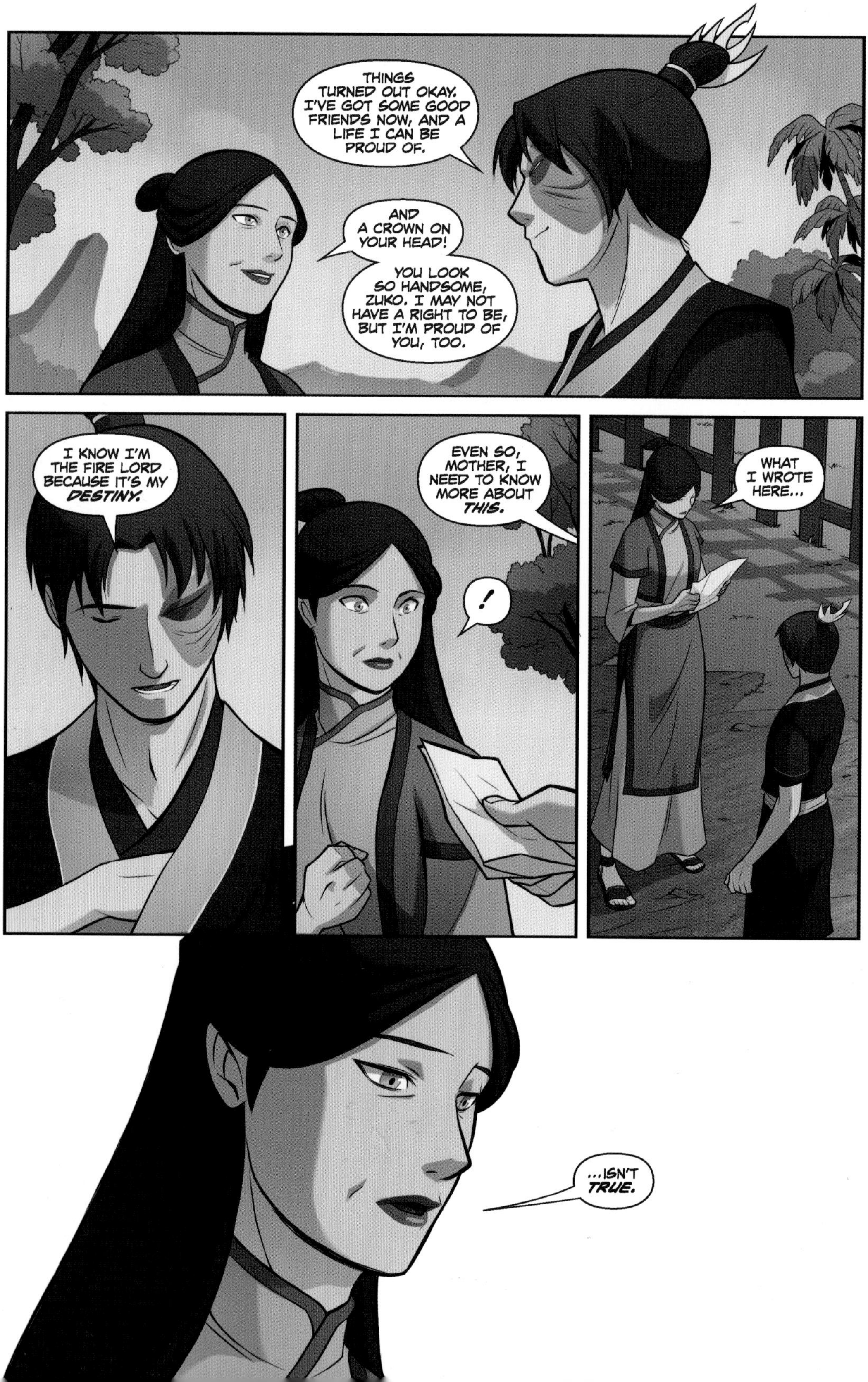

THINGS TURNED OUT OKAY. I'VE GOT SOME GOOD FRIENDS NOW, AND A LIFE I CAN BE PROUD OF.
AND A CROWN ON YOUR HEAD!
YOU LOOK SO HANDSOME, ZUKO. I MAY NOT HAVE A RIGHT TO BE, BUT I'M PROUD OF YOU, TOO.
I KNOW I'M THE FIRE LORD BECAUSE IT'S MY *DESTINY.*
EVEN SO, MOTHER, I NEED TO KNOW MORE ABOUT *THIS.*
!
WHAT I WROTE HERE...
...ISN'T *TRUE.*

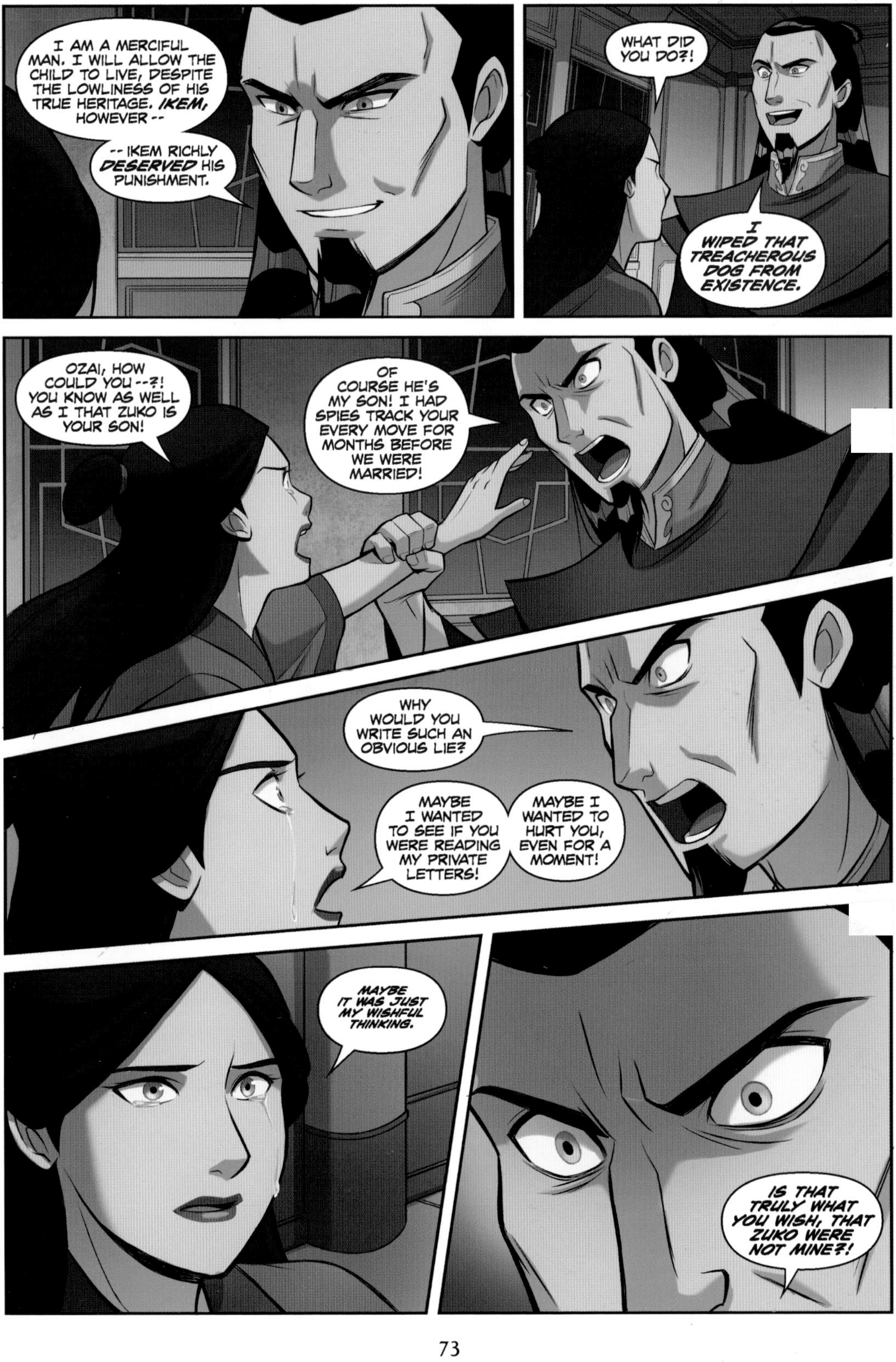
I AM A MERCIFUL MAN. I WILL ALLOW THE CHILD TO LIVE, DESPITE THE LOWLINESS OF HIS TRUE HERITAGE. IKEM, HOWEVER --
-- IKEM RICHLY DESERVED HIS PUNISHMENT.
WHAT DID YOU DO?!
I WIPED THAT TREACHEROUS DOG FROM EXISTENCE.
OZAI, HOW COULD YOU --?! YOU KNOW AS WELL AS I THAT ZUKO IS YOUR SON!
OF COURSE HE'S MY SON! I HAD SPIES TRACK YOUR EVERY MOVE FOR MONTHS BEFORE WE WERE MARRIED!
WHY WOULD YOU WRITE SUCH AN OBVIOUS LIE?
MAYBE I WANTED TO SEE IF YOU WERE READING MY PRIVATE LETTERS!
MAYBE I WANTED TO HURT YOU, EVEN FOR A MOMENT!
MAYBE IT WAS JUST MY WISHFUL THINKING.
IS THAT TRULY WHAT YOU WISH, THAT ZUKO WERE NOT MINE?!

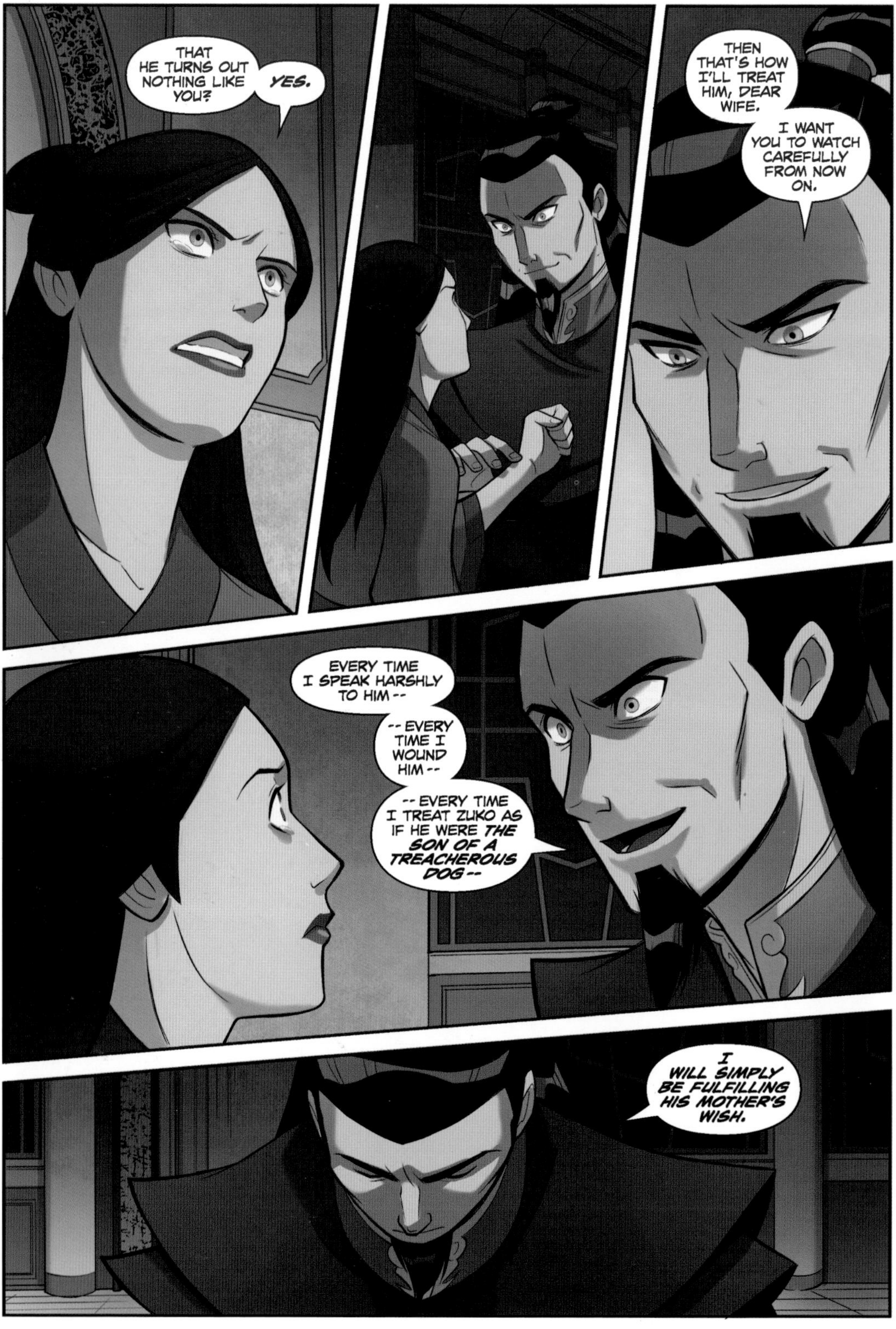
THAT HE TURNS OUT NOTHING LIKE YOU?
YES.
THEN THAT'S HOW I'LL TREAT HIM, DEAR WIFE.
I WANT YOU TO WATCH CAREFULLY FROM NOW ON.
EVERY TIME I SPEAK HARSHLY TO HIM --
-- EVERY TIME I WOUND HIM --
-- EVERY TIME I TREAT ZUKO AS IF HE WERE THE SON OF A TREACHEROUS DOG --
I WILL SIMPLY BE FULFILLING HIS MOTHER'S WISH.

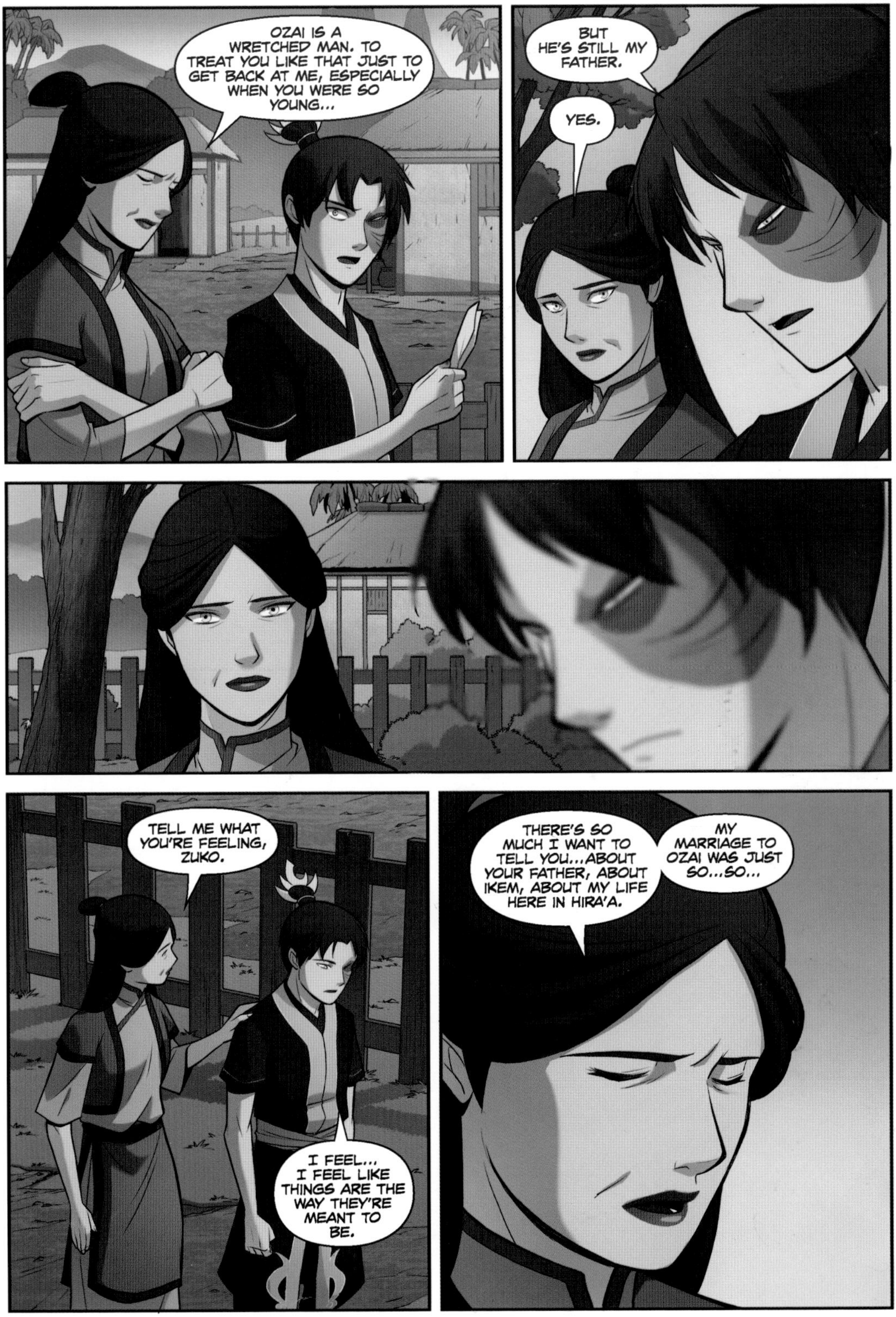
OZAI IS A WRETCHED MAN. TO TREAT YOU LIKE THAT JUST TO GET BACK AT ME, ESPECIALLY WHEN YOU WERE SO YOUNG...
BUT HE'S STILL MY FATHER.
YES.
TELL ME WHAT YOU'RE FEELING, ZUKO.
I FEEL... I FEEL LIKE THINGS ARE THE WAY THEY'RE MEANT TO BE.
THERE'S SO MUCH I WANT TO TELL YOU...ABOUT YOUR FATHER, ABOUT IKEM, ABOUT MY LIFE HERE IN HIRA'A.
MY MARRIAGE TO OZAI WAS JUST SO...SO...

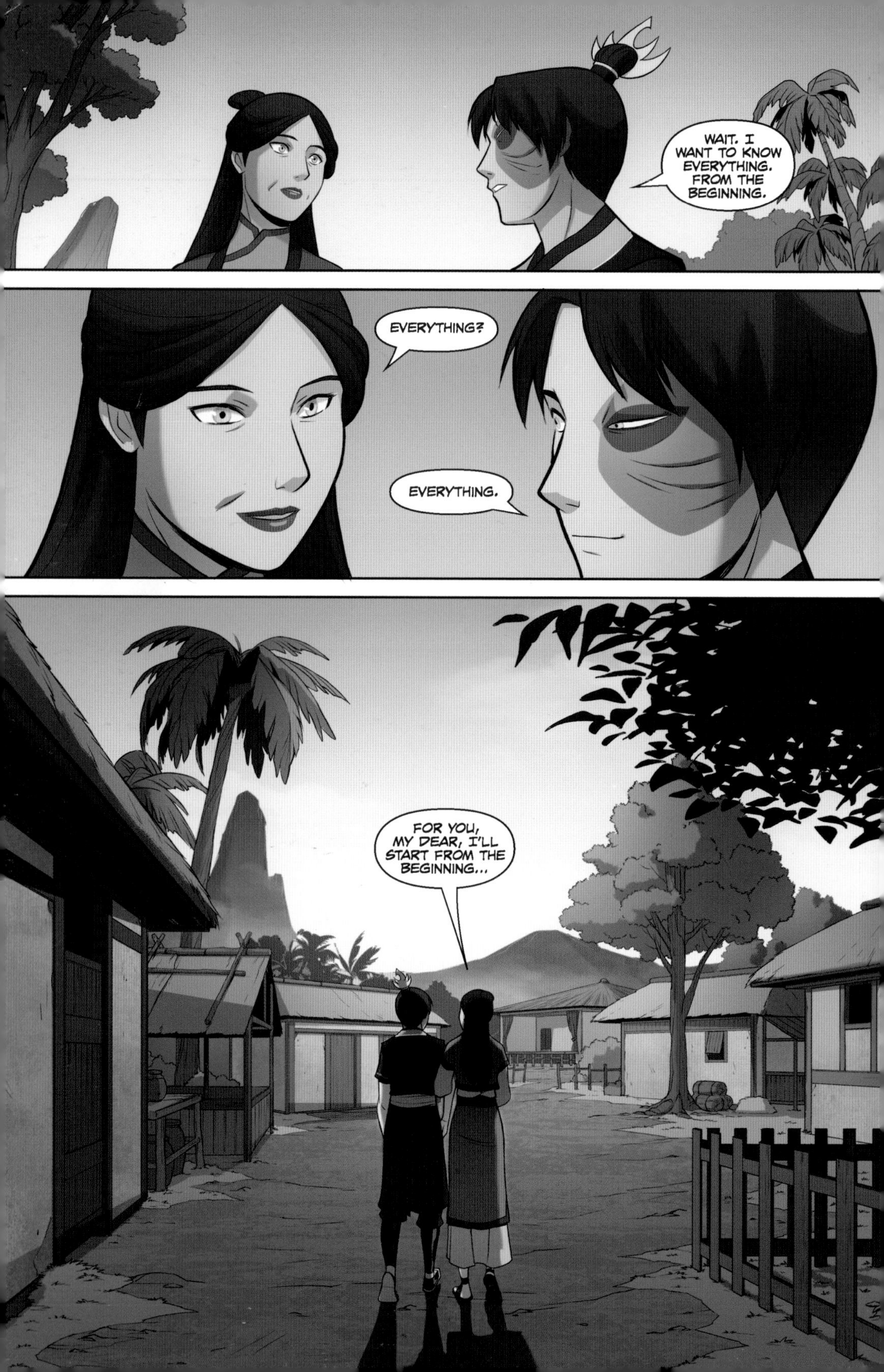
WAIT. I WANT TO KNOW EVERYTHING. FROM THE BEGINNING.
EVERYTHING?
EVERYTHING.
FOR YOU, MY DEAR, I'LL START FROM THE BEGINNING...

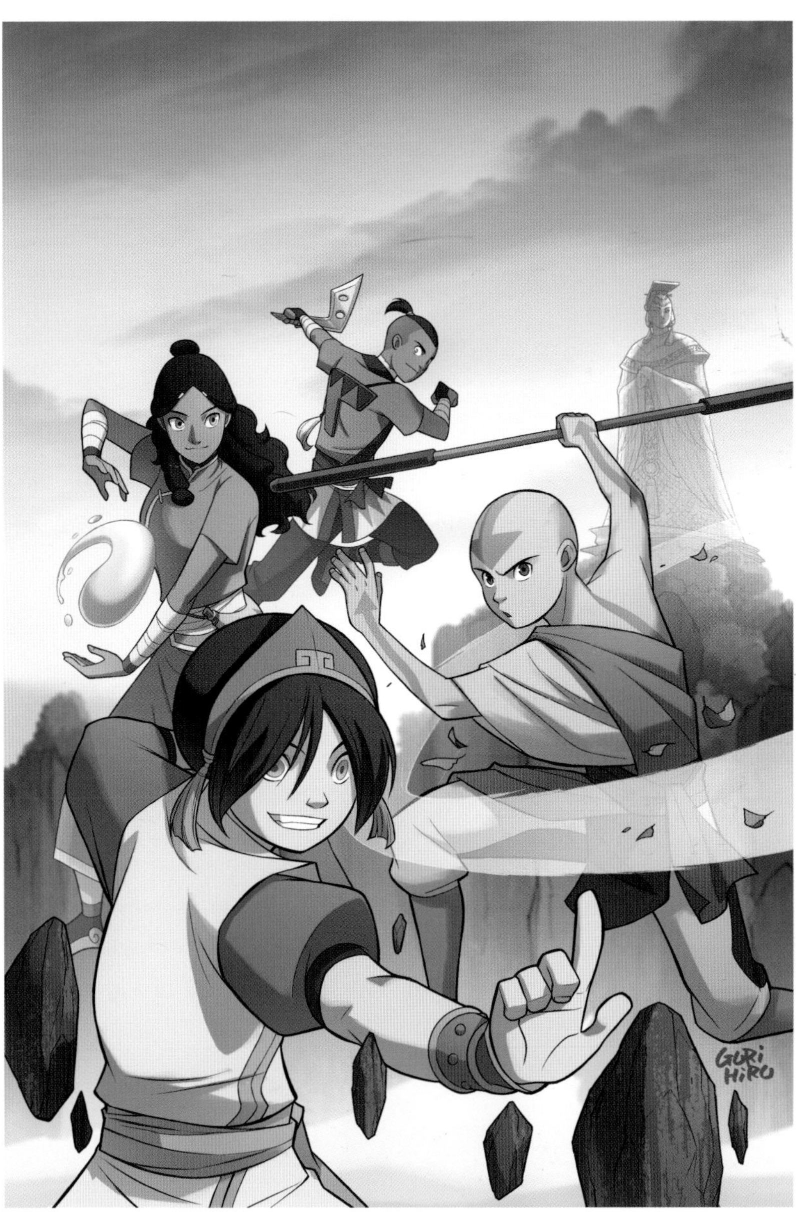
GURIHIRU

## COMING IN MARCH

Aang uncovers a terrible secret in . . .

**THE RIFT • PART ONE**

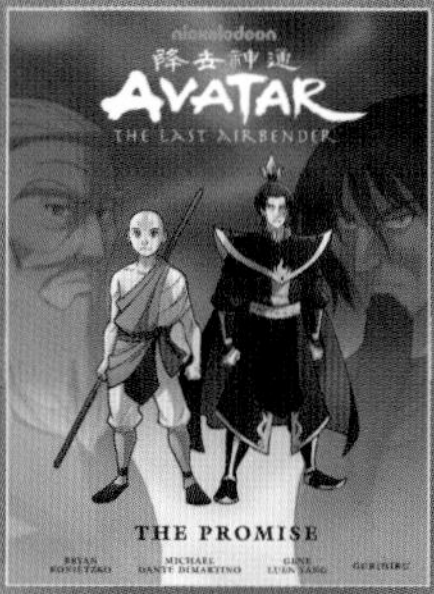
nickelodeon
降去神通
AVATAR
THE LAST AIRBENDER
THE PROMISE

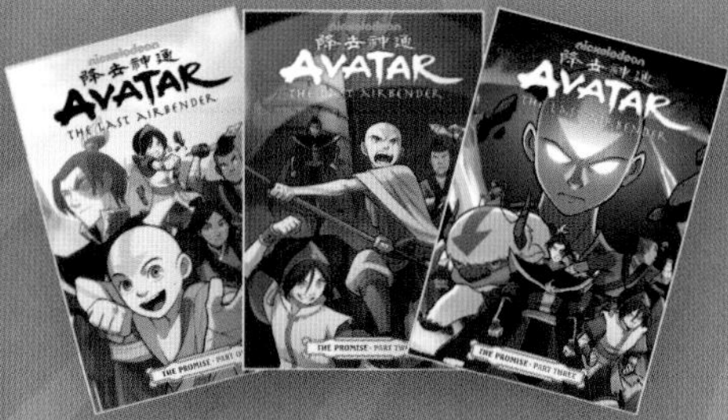
AVATAR
THE LAST AIRBENDER

Avatar: The Last Airbender—
The Promise Library Edition
978-1-61655-074-5 $39.99

Avatar: The Last Airbender—
The Promise Part 1
978-1-59582-811-8 $10.99

Avatar: The Last Airbender—
The Promise Part 2
978-1-59582-875-0 $10.99

Avatar: The Last Airbender—
The Promise Part 3
978-1-59582-941-2 $10.99

Avatar: The Last Airbender—
The Search Library Edition
978-1-61655-226-8 $39.99

Avatar: The Last Airbender—
The Search Part 1
978-1-61655-054-7 $10.99

Avatar: The Last Airbender—
The Search Part 2
978-1-61655-190-2 $10.99

Avatar: The Last Airbender—
The Search Part 3
978-1-61655-184-1 $10.99

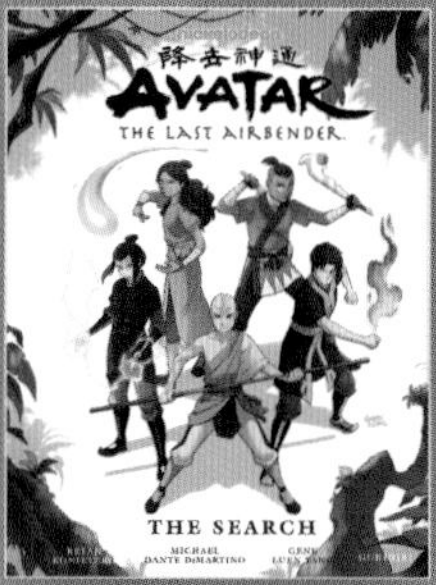
降去神通
AVATAR
THE LAST AIRBENDER
THE SEARCH

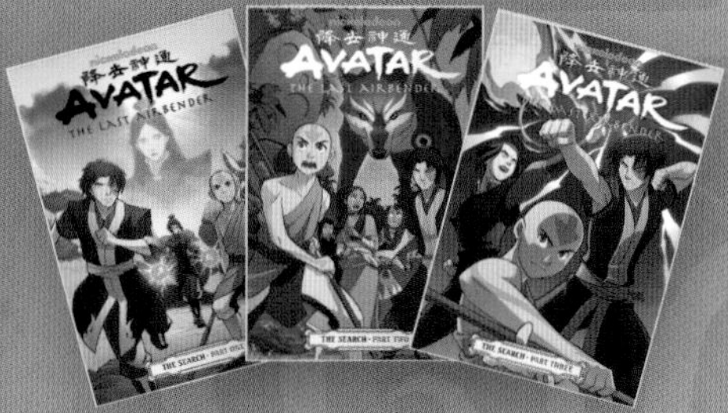
AVATAR
THE LAST AIRBENDER

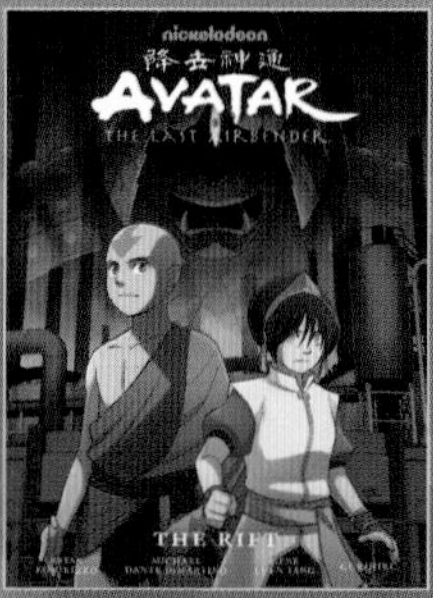
nickelodeon
降去神通
AVATAR
THE LAST AIRBENDER
THE RIFT

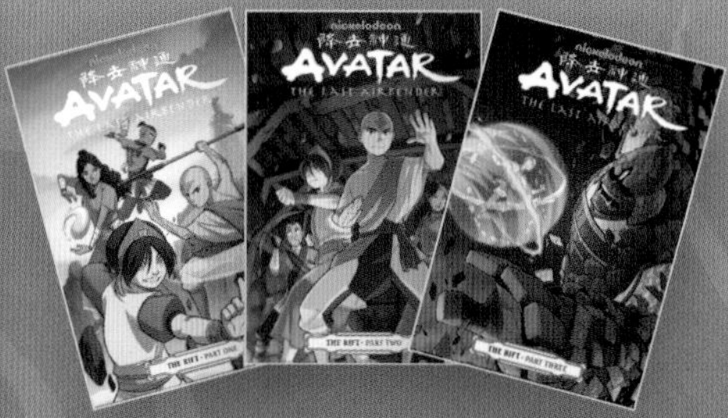
AVATAR
THE LAST AIRBENDER

Avatar: The Last Airbender—
The Rift Library Edition
978-1-61655-550-4 $39.99

Avatar: The Last Airbender—
The Rift Part 1
978-1-61655-295-4 $10.99

Avatar: The Last Airbender—
The Rift Part 2
978-1-61655-296-1 $10.99

Avatar: The Last Airbender—
The Rift Part 3
978-1-61655-297-8 $10.99

Avatar: The Last Airbender—
Smoke and Shadow Library
Edition
978-1-50670-013-7 $39.99

Avatar: The Last Airbender—
Smoke and Shadow Part 1
978-1-61655-761-4 $10.99

Avatar: The Last Airbender—
Smoke and Shadow Part 2
978-1-61655-790-4 $10.99

Avatar: The Last Airbender—
Smoke and Shadow Part 3
978-1-61655-838-3 $10.99

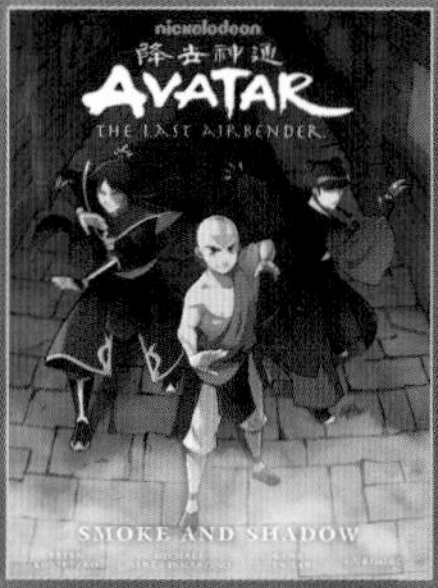
nickelodeon
降去神通
AVATAR
THE LAST AIRBENDER
SMOKE AND SHADOW

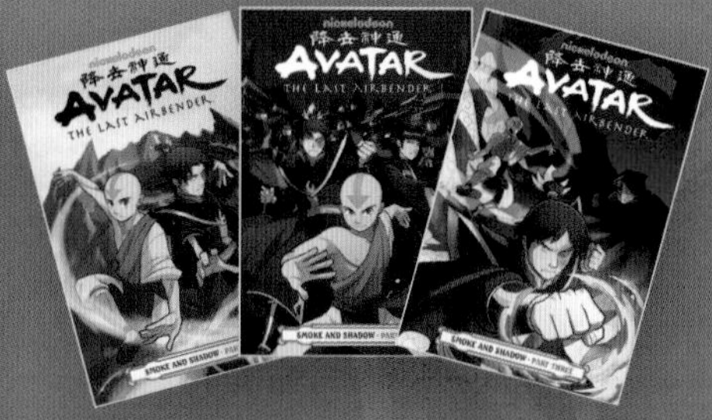
AVATAR
THE LAST AIRBENDER